This book is essential reading for any teacher interested in making science learning more meaningful and lasting. Joan Gallagher-Bolos and Dennis Smithenry show us classrooms in which teens take responsibility for their learning as they engage with problems—connecting ideas, working together, learning how to ask questions, and evaluating their own progress. Rather than absorbing disconnected facts, the students participate in a scientific community, with all the excitement, learning, and challenge that it implies.

—Bertram C. Bruce
University of Illinois at Urbana-Champaign

Now, with Teaching Inquiry-Based Chemistry, *teachers have exciting new methods that will challenge their students to become critical thinkers and independent learners. The authors present science educators with innovations that transform classrooms and students, all in a book that is informative, witty, and immensely readable.*

—Mike Schroeder, Ph.D.
Augustana College
Coauthor, *Constructivist Methods for the Secondary Classroom*

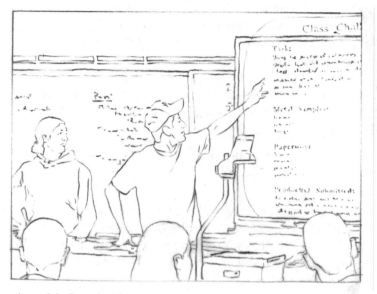

Artwork by Doug Smithenry

Teaching Inquiry-Based Chemistry

Creating Student-Led Scientific Communities

Joan A. Gallagher-Bolos

Dennis W. Smithenry, Ph.D.

HEINEMANN
Portsmouth, NH

Heinemann
A division of Reed Elsevier Inc.
361 Hanover Street
Portsmouth, NH 03801–3912
www.heinemann.com

Offices and agents throughout the world

The author and publisher wish to thank those who have generously given permission to reprint borrowed material: Student journal entries courtesy of Jessica Poter and Kristen Horsey.

Library of Congress Cataloging-in-Publication Data
Gallagher-Bolos, Joan A.
   Teaching inquiry-based chemistry : creating student-led scientific communities /
   Joan A. Gallagher-Bolos and Dennis W. Smithenry.
      p. cm.
   ISBN 0-325-00671-7 (alk. paper)
   1. Chemistry—Study and teaching (Secondary)—United States.
I. Smithenry, Dennis W. II. Title.
QD40.G32 2004
540'.7'12—dc22   2004010431

Editor: Robin Najar
Production coordinator: Sonja S. Chapman
Production service: Lisa S. Garboski, bookworks
Cover design: Night & Day Design
Compositor: Reuben Kantor, QEP
Manufacturing: Steve Bernier

America on acid-free paper
2   3   4   5

For my twin brother, Doug, who grew up with the same need to be creative.

Dennis

For my husband, Spiro, whose unending support, encouragement, sacrifice, intelligence, and friendship made this book possible. Thank you.

For my daughters, Katina and Kira, who have taught me more about teaching and learning than anyone else in the world. Never stop asking questions, girls!

Joan

Contents

This chapter describes how to set up an intriguing classroom that resembles what was described in the last chapter. We explain how to start preparing students for the culminating activity by showing the teacher how to develop a self-sufficient scientific community. We illustrate this process by sharing activities that appropriately begin the journey.

These stories and activities focus on what to do during the first couple weeks of the school year. The chapter is divided into sections, each discussing the five important aspects to building this community so that it will function successfully, with or without the teacher's guidance—climate, trust, safety, journals, and cooperation.

This chapter details and compares projects that are done at different points during the school year. We illustrate numerous activities and projects that require students to collaborate in order to develop a justifiable and/or quality product. These projects also describe how to slowly and methodically hand the reins over to the students, getting out of their way so meaningful educational experiences can take place.

Foreword

One thing we have learned in over sixty collective years of teaching at levels varying from middle school to a large university is that students learn best when they are intimately involved in the process. In contrast, "talking at" students (lecturing) is one of the least effective ways to convey understanding. There is no doubt in our minds that true understanding of a concept is constructed by each individual in his/her brain. This "constructivist" learning only occurs effectively when the student is participating in a meaningful way in the learning process. We call this "active learning" and we believe this is by far the best way to achieve effective learning. Active learning is at its best when the students are actually responsible for their own learning with only minimal guidance from the teacher.

This delightful book exudes contagious enthusiasm for active learning that will inspire virtually any teacher to begin teaching this way and encourage those who have already used active learning in some way to venture even further down this path. Teaching in this style is difficult at first because it is so different from the way that most of us were taught. It is hard to actually let students make mistakes and find their own way through problems and situations. It is also scary at first because we worry about whether we are teaching enough content to prepare the students for increasing numbers of standardized exams and for college. Our experience is that teaching content with little understanding of the underlying concepts is almost useless in the long run. Helping students to learn to think creatively, communicate, and work in teams is much more important than having them memorize lists of facts or rules. But creative thinking is not something that you can give to your students. They must learn it on their own and one of the best ways for them to do this is to make mistakes and figure out how to correct their mistakes on their own. Interrupting the exploration process by correcting students as soon as they start down the "wrong" road is one of the worst things a teacher can do. Let the students learn from their own mistakes. Closely related is the effectiveness of peer teaching. Why did we all learn so much in our first years of teaching? We found our misconceptions when we couldn't explain something to our students, and we fixed them by reading a text or talking to a colleague. This same thing happens in student groups as they attempt to solve a problem together.

The authors of this book understand the power of active learning and convey it effectively with enthusiasm and specific examples to help you do it in your own classroom. We hope you enjoy the stories, understand the frustrations, and become enthused about turning your classroom over to your students in many ways as you read this book.

—Susan and Steven Zumdahl

Introduction

During our first few years of teaching, we remember being drained and frustrated with how little students seemed to care about learning. They weren't concerned with being actively involved in experiencing science. It became apparent that somewhere in the past, they were conditioned to believe that textbooks and recipe-driven labs define science. They thought that all the questions had been asked and answered, and therefore their only job was to learn the facts. Because they had no ownership of the problems presented to them, they didn't want to apply the information. They acted like robots.

We didn't want this type of class climate. So we asked ourselves, "What can we do to motivate students to get involved, to want to learn, to be curious about what's being presented?" After a good deal of experimenting in the classroom with different teaching methods, we realized that when we introduced a project where the students had freedom and responsibility, they became active participants and actually enjoyed science! Our focus question then became, "Who's running our classroom?" We knew that if the students were running things instead of us, they would become involved.

So we slowly put them in charge by gradually handing over the reins to the students as the year progressed. We now have active participants taking lessons above and beyond where we ever expected them to go. Instead of robotic learners, we observe:

- Students who own their science experience
- Students who are responsible for the final outcome of all activities, including lab planning, experimentation, analysis of data, and presentations of conclusions
- Students who learn to use freedom constructively in a group setting

- Students who further develop their talents and improve on weaknesses
- Students who develop a well-rounded definition for science
- Students who have fun *doing* science

While writing curricula and implementing activities that build a self-sufficient scientific community, we have found ourselves to be:

- Teachers who act as guides rather than disseminators of information
- Teachers who step outside of traditional teacher roles
- Teachers who are comfortable allowing their students to make decisions
- Teachers who have fun

We have created the classroom described above in eight unique school districts throughout our teaching careers. We (Dennis and Joan) have collaborated on curriculum development for the past nine years, though we have taught in the same district only one year. The districts in which we have taught included the full spectrum of schools: inner city, suburban, upper-middle class, small population (200 students), large population (2800 students), etc. We have also seen these classrooms come alive at every level of science, from freshmen physical science to senior-level advanced placement chemistry. So it can be used in any school and in any classroom.

Our book is structured in five parts, each section sharing a selection of our teaching stories. This book describes the implementation of activities that slowly shift the balance of who's in charge, from teacher to student, as the school year progresses. The benefits of allowing the students to be in charge are explained with each story. Our overall goal is to illustrate how we've motivated the students to take an active role in their science experience, thus creating the classroom atmosphere described earlier.

SEPT	*Scientific Community*
OCT	*Part. Nature of Matter & Gas Laws*
NOV	*Atomic Structure & Per. Trends*
DEC	*Reactions & Stoich.*
JAN	*Stoich.*
FEB	*Equilibrium & Thermo-chemistry*
MAR	*Acids & Bases*
APR	*Organic*
MAY	*Soap* — *Soap Project*
JUNE	*Finals*

1
How Did We Get Here?

It's 3:10 P.M. Joan walks into Dennis' classroom just as his class is leaving. "Man, Joan, they wore me out today. I can't even think! They were so upset about getting homework the night of prom. They know that I always give homework. Why would it be different just because it's prom weekend? They just wouldn't let it drop."

Joan starts to grin.

"No way, Joan!" Dennis exclaims in disbelief. "You didn't give them homework? Oh, well, at least my strict rigid demeanor remains intact!"

Now Joan laughs slyly. "Why would anyone give homework for prom night? I choose my battles wisely." And then she sits down and again asks, "So what's our next unit? We're done with acids/bases. We've only got four weeks left until summer. Let's think of an overall project for them. Any ideas?"

Dennis thinks for a minute. "Well, I did do this week-long project during student teaching. I developed it in a graduate course and I really wanted to try it out. I took a soap lab from a chemistry lab manual and applied the constructivist theory to it, by requiring the students to investigate how to make soap, as opposed to giving them a recipe. I think that I called it a 'miniature scientific community.'" Dennis laughs, finishes shuffling the mound of papers on the desk, sits in the "teacher" stool, and stares at Joan. "Is that the type of thing you're talking about?"

She says, "Exactly. How did it work?"

"Well, I threw the idea out to the students that their job as a class was to attempt to do a chemistry fundraiser by producing and marketing soap to the school student body. I brainstormed the criteria for a successful fundraiser with the students, and we came up with a list. They needed to make a packaged soap prototype, do a marketing survey of the student body, complete a cost analysis of whether we could make money with such an endeavor, and videotape a commercial for our product. I remember that one student came back the next day with stories from his grandmother of how they used to make soap as kids. It was so much fun! I remember stepping back and watching them go."

"That sounds like fun! Let's do even more. What if we made each of our classes a separate soap company where there were science and business divisions each with managers? And the soap companies could compete against one another." Joan begins to get animated.

"Yeah, and in the science division we could have engineers and research scientists. The research scientists could be doing small-scale testing of soap recipes and the engineers' job would be to scale up the production of the best recipe. It'll be just like industry," Dennis adds, catching the thread of Joan's energy.

"And the managers would totally be in charge of their companies. They would have to make daily decisions on what needs to be accomplished. We could 'disappear' for a week or so and role-play as different characters from OSHA or FDA in order to check up on their progress! OK, cool, Dennis. This sounds great. Let's hash it out!" Dennis laughs and agrees.

We then spend the evening sketching outlines and brainstorming ideas for how this project might actually work.

Hence, the soap project was born. The above dialogue is a rendition of the quick initial conversation that resulted in the culminating activity described in Chapter 2. Some of the greatest activities we've ever come up with were developed by taking a simple lab activity and going crazy with it. We step out of the box. We brainstorm ideas on how to turn the recipe-written lab into a problem that the students need to solve. We throw in industry-based tasks whenever possible so that the class needs to work as a scientific research community. The end result is a legitimate inquiry-based lab.

We're sharing the birth of our most complicated project to date because we want you to know how it is that we came to write this book. However, this project was not born on that particular day, but came from our collaborating on smaller, similar projects throughout the year. The reason for our innovative approach to labs/projects was rooted in the movement in the early 1990s in education toward a constructivist-based classroom. The soap project was a natural conclusion to the small projects we had developed all year.

> "Oh, my God, it's eight at night already. Let's get out of here and go grab some food and a drink. Get all the scraps of paper so we can keep working on this."
>
> We head to the local tavern and continue brainstorming our newly designed soap project. We write on anything available, including napkins and coasters, so that no detail is left unrecorded. We get to the point where we have all the job descriptions written, the project sheet outlined, a tentative calendar prepared, and their first assignment of a job resumé ready for tomorrow. When we're finished, it's so late that it's last call.

The result of our endeavors is shown by Handout 1—Soap Project Sheet (1st Draft). This is our first draft of the soap project that we gave to our students the following Monday. (The most recent version of this project is shown in Chapter 2.)

Handout 1—Soap Project Sheet (1st Draft)

Project objectives

1. Improve communication skills
   - Operating in a scientific community
   - Defining target audience
   - Formulating concise, objective-oriented memos
2. Experience a real-life scientific endeavor
   - Understanding what scientists do
   - Learning one chemical process for producing something
3. Become familiar with the corporate world
   - Experiencing how different teams interact to accomplish a desired goal
   - Learning how to function under time, monetary, and regulatory constraints

Initial class activities

    Day 1—As a class, we need to find out how to make soap.
        How is soap made?
        What should the pH of soap be?
    Day 2—Decision on soap recipe to use.
    Day 3—Make an initial product, turn in resumé.
    Day 4—Give folder for portfolio.
        Each team has a leader, secretary, and representative to report
            daily to the CEO.
        Class becomes a company.

Team tasks, goals, and identity

1. CEO—CORPORATE EXECUTIVE OFFICER
    Provides direction based on information given from teams below.
    All teams must report to CEO.
    All major decisions made by CEO.
    Has a vested interest in all that happens because s/he represents
        the company.
    Calls daily meetings with team representative for status reports.
    CEO reports to OSHA, FDA, EPA.

2. ENGINEERS
    Deal with equipment.
    Bring small scale to large scale on paper and in lab.
    Work out the bugs in the process.
    Report on feasibility of large-scale production to accounting (eco-
        nomics, equipment).
    Use results from research scientists to continually update their
        plan for large-scale production.

3. RESEARCH SCIENTISTS
    Take public relations ideas to see if the products can be made on a
        small scale.
    Plan and perform experiments necessary to check possibilities.
    Document experiments and results.
    Must keep engineers informed of results.

4. ACCOUNTING
All financial transactions documented.
Consolidates all other expenditures and reports to CEO.
Finds out average yearly salaries for team members.
Pays weekly salaries.

5. MARKETING
Comes up with marketing campaign.
Marketing strategies (packaging, advertising campaign, distribution, commercials [videos], posters, spies).

6. PUBLIC RELATIONS
What does the consumer want?
Sample survey with consumers (school students).
Gets consumers to the marketing posters.
Spies—how other companies are campaigning, and how consumers are responding to those campaigns.
Reports consumer demands to research scientists.

7. QUALITY CONTROL
Checks the safety of the product for consumer use.
(Tests for pH level of products from both research scientists and engineers.)
Checks for uniformity, appearance, and consistency of product from engineers.
Provides testing reports to marketing, engineers, and research scientists.

8. OSHA, FDA, EPA
- Occupational Safety and Health Administration
- Food and Drug Administration
- Environmental Protection Agency
  We are the monkey wrench in your plans!
  We will make unannounced visits to ensure that all regulations and codes are being met. We can shut down your operations for the day and/or impose fines.
  We will write compliance checklist if fines are imposed.

Grading

Participation grades. On-task behavior means you're in character. Your portfolio will be compared to like teams from other classes in terms of completing the preceding tasks and goals.

Reading this assignment sheet eight years later, we are still amazed that we went ahead and took the risk to try the activity, not knowing at all what the outcome might be. This was a bare-bones assignment with minimal direction. But upon further reflection, we feel that our backgrounds gave us the confidence to take the risk and see the project through. During the 1994–95 school year, Dennis was a first-year teacher full of idealism, thoroughly worn out by the demands of the job, yet still wanting to try the lessons he had developed as a student teacher. Joan was an experienced teacher in her seventh year willing and able to take risks and try out new ideas for the benefit of her students, even though there was department pressure not to do so.

Having met in the summer prior to this school year, we sat down and discussed our teaching philosophies. We found that we shared a common belief in the benefits of applying the constructivist theory to our teaching practice. So early on, we were committed to developing a chemistry curriculum that shifted the emphasis from teacher-centered lecture/lab/test instruction to one that incorporated an inquiry spirit driven by the students. In addition, a reform movement was taking place across the country that called for exactly that kind of shift. The American Association for the Advancement of Science had published *Science for All Americans*, a book that advocated inquiry teaching as a method for increasing scientific literacy for students. Dennis' previous certification and graduate science education courses were saturated with the constructivist theory. Preservice science teachers were being challenged to implement the constructivist theory into their new classrooms. And in 1996, science educators were given the *National Science Education Standards* (NSES) where a clear call, based on research, was made to make inquiry teaching a priority in science classrooms. It was so important that this was followed up in the year 2000 with an entire book called *Inquiry and the National Science Education Standards*. Our teaching practices described in this book contain this inquiry spirit and are fully supported by the standards outlined in the NSES books.

Thus, with these ideas as a backdrop, we developed the year-long chemistry curriculum that we have outlined in this book. And the cornerstone of this curriculum became the soap project. We found that it was where we wanted our students to be at the end of the year, and what we wanted to prepare them for during the eight months preceding.

> During the first week of the first year of doing the soap project, Joan flies into the prep room and in a panic-stricken voice yells at Dennis, "They have no soap! None of them. None of my companies have soap. They've had a full week. They have no soap yet! What are we going to do? Have you seen the stuff in their molds? They only have four more days! Dennis, *they have no soap!*"
>
> Dennis chuckles and says, "Yeah, my classes have no soap, either. Soap is hard to make. I told you that." After Joan threatens to hit him, he gets serious. "But you're right, what should we do? They have to have something to turn in next week."
>
> We walk around the lab room looking at all the samples of what is supposed to be soap. Most of them look like mashed potatoes. None of them are safe to touch. Dennis says, "Here's a slogan for this company, 'Our soap gets you so clean, it gets under your skin.'" We lose it. We're laughing hysterically. We're past the panic and relax a bit. Then we sit down to brainstorm.
>
> "OK, we can still salvage this. So far, they've been frustrated, but all their setbacks have been exactly what I experienced in industry. They are truly living the life of an engineer," Dennis says.
>
> "OK, this is good. This has been a good experience for them. They're figuring out—on their own—what's wrong with what's wrong. We're gonna have to type up some lengthy feedback for them when this is all over so they know how to view these experiences positively," Joan responds.
>
> "I think so, too," Dennis says. "But let's focus on how to help them get to the next step without giving them too much guidance. We could role-play as somebody . . ."
>
> Joan jumps in. "Let's come in as a board member of the company or something, wanting to find out their progress. Maybe our questions will help them figure out where to focus their energy."
>
> "Awesome! Let's make a list of what we'll ask when we come in. You know I need organized lesson plans," Dennis jokes.

Even the best-made plans, written neatly on paper—those that parallel perfectly what the standards say, those that parallel what our gut tells us is in the best interests of the students—may seem ridiculously lost during implementation. Yet we found comfort and sanity when we worked together in these moments of frustration. It was during these times that we ironed out the details and decided how to move forward. What helps us maintain focus is to know going into a project that we will experience moments of doubt.

We have found that there are two key ingredients to trying any one of these inquiry-based projects:

- Be willing to stick it out.
- Spend a good amount of time on evaluations/reflections/feedback with the students once it's over.

We have never given up on a project midstream no matter how frustrating things may appear on a given day. If we did, we are certain that the students would not put forth their best effort in the future because they would think they could talk us out of finishing it. So instead of despairing, we find that there's always a way to bring the kids back on the right track with a few modifications made the next day of class. The following is an illustration of the teacher role-playing as one of the company stockholders. The teacher asks some guiding questions of Kristen, the student who has been assigned as the class' (company's) CEO of the soap company. In doing so, she gives Kristen the help she needs to get the class back on track.

> "Hello, Kristen. My name is Ms. Smith. I'm a member of the stockholders' board of trustees. I just stopped by to find out how things are going with you. Can you bring me up to speed?" Joan asks the company CEO.
>
> Kristen is caught off-guard. It's been a while since she's had to "answer" to anyone. Finally she says, hesitantly, "Well, I'll be honest. We've had a few problems and I'm trying to decide what to tell my workers to do today."
>
> "Well, I used to be in your position. Why don't we spend a couple minutes brainstorming together to see if we can come up with a plan? That way, I can tell the other board members that things are OK."

Kristen leads "Ms. Smith" to her "office," a desk in the corner of the room. Ms. Smith then asks, "Let's start with the science wing. What have they accomplished?"

"Well," Kristen says, pulling out some papers with notes written on them, "they've done quite a few small-scale trials. Trial 3 had good results, meaning I thought it was the best sample of soap so far. So my engineers upscaled it and it was total mush. We don't know what to do next."

Ms. Smith says, "Have you had the research scientists sit down with the engineers to go through their changes to see if they catch any errors? And have you had any of the scientists doing research on the upscale process? What do they need to think about? Is there anyone 'out there' who has tried this and had similar results? These are the places I would start."

"Okay. Should I go tell them now?" Kristen asks.

"First you should get down a few questions that you need answered by these workers. Brainstorming with your science leaders might be good. So take ten minutes to do this and then get your science wing busy. What about the business end?"

Ms. Smith and Kristen talk about what roadblocks exist in the business section of the company. Ms. Smith gives her some suggestions on what questions to focus on and then leaves. It's in Kristen's capable hands . . . again.

Not all classes need this kind of guidance. And some classes will need a bit more. It depends on the makeup of the class and how they've developed as the year progresses. We decide per class what type of guidance is needed and plan accordingly. This class just needed a quick push in the right direction. Our biggest concern is that we always maintain the integrity of the project by erring on the side of being conservative with our input.

Once the soap project was completed this first year, Dennis and I forced ourselves to sit down and rewrite the project sheets so that they would "work better" the next year. We put in details or reworded parts of the project sheets in order to improve them for the next year. Now we actually do this for every project we do so that the following year we'll remember what it was that we thought would make a better challenge for our students. A copy of the revamped project sheet that we handed out at the end of the 1995–96 school year, Handout 2—IT'S CLEANUP TIME! (1st Revision), follows.

Handout 2—It's Cleanup Time! (1st Revision)

Project objectives

1. Improve communication skills
   - Operating in a scientific community
   - Defining target audience
   - Formulating concise, objective-oriented memos

2. Experience a real-life scientific endeavor
   - Understanding what scientists do
   - Learning one chemical process for producing something

3. Become familiar with the corporate world
   - Experiencing how different teams interact to accomplish a desired goal
   - Learning how to function under time, monetary, and regulatory constraints

Task

   - As a class we will figure out how soap is made. We will be researching in the library on Tuesday and Wednesday on the following questions. If you would like to do any individual research before Tuesday, that will help your company.
   - What recipe can you find for making soap? How much soap does the recipe produce? How does soap work? What should the pH of soap be? Anything else you think will be important in helping your team accomplish its goals (see below).
   - We will then, as a class, choose and use a recipe to make an initial soap product in the lab on Thursday and Friday.
   - Our desired goal is to end up with 2 pounds of quality soap.

Job vacancies! Apply now!

We (the class) are an existing company based in Elmhurst, Illinois, that plans to enter the market of producing soap. Each of our departments in turn needs to hire more people in order to handle the production of this new product. Please read the job openings available below. If you are interested in applying for any of these positions, please submit a resumé by Monday, May 8th. If you have a first and second choice, please note that on the resumé. (If you do not have a preference and do not choose to submit a resumé, a position will be assigned to you.) You should note that since these research teams will be working for three weeks only, no sick days are allowed. Being absent means a pay deduction.

Team tasks, goals, and identity

1. CEO—CHIEF EXECUTIVE OFFICER (3)

   Must choose a leader, a secretary, and a representative to report daily to group 8.

   Provides direction based on information given from teams below.

   All teams must report to CEO.

   All major decisions made by CEO.

   Has a vested interest in all that happens because these three represent the company.

   Calls daily meetings with team representative for status reports.

   CEO reports to OSHA, FDA, EPA.

   Documents everything on a daily basis.

2. ENGINEERS (4–6)

   Must choose a leader, a secretary, and a representative to report daily to CEO team.

   Deal with equipment.

   Bring small scale to large scale on paper and in lab.

   Work out the bugs in the process.

   Keep record of all expenditures.

   Use results from research scientists to continually update their plan for large-scale production.

   Report on feasibility of large-scale production to research scientists and accounting (economics, equipment)

3. RESEARCH SCIENTISTS (4–6)

   Must choose a leader, a secretary, and a representative to report daily to CEO team.

   Take public relations ideas to see if the products can be made on a small scale.

   Plan and perform experiments necessary to check possibilities.

Keep record of all expenditures.

Document experiments and results.

Must keep engineers informed of results.

4. ACCOUNTING (3)

Must choose a leader, a secretary, and a representative to report daily to CEO team.

All financial transactions documented.

Consolidates all other expenditures and reports to CEO.

Finds out average yearly salaries for team members.

Pays weekly salaries. (Do not pay group 8.) This means you have to keep track of attendance on a daily basis. Taxes—state, social security, and federal—need to be deducted. Report to CEOs.

5. MARKETING AND ADVERTISING (3–5)

Must choose a leader, a secretary, and a representative to report daily to CEO team.

Comes up with marketing campaign.

Keeps record of all expenditures.

Marketing strategies (packaging, advertising campaign, distribution, commercials [videos], posters, spies).

Consults with public relations to ensure that marketing campaign is in line with consumer wants.

6. PUBLIC RELATIONS (3–5)

Must choose a leader, a secretary, and a representative to report daily to CEO team.

What does the consumer want?

Sample survey with consumers (school students).

Gets consumers to the marketing posters.

Keeps record of all expenditures.

Spies—how other companies are campaigning, and how consumers are responding to those campaigns.

Reports consumer demands to research scientists.

Consults with marketing to give ideas for campaign.

7. QUALITY CONTROL (3)

Must choose a leader, a secretary, and a representative to report daily to CEO team.

Checks the safety of the product for consumer use.

(Tests for pH level of products from both research scientists and engineers.)

Checks for uniformity, appearance, and consistency of product from engineers.

Keeps record of all expenditures.

Provides testing reports to marketing, engineers, research scientists, and FDA.

8. OSHA, FDA, EPA (Sorry, these positions are already filled.)
   - Occupational Safety and Health Administration
   - Food and Drug Administration
   - Environmental Protection Agency

   We are the monkey wrench in your plans!

   We will make unannounced visits to ensure that all regulations and codes are being met. We can shut down your operations for the day and/or impose fines.

   We will write compliance checklist if fines are imposed.

9. COMPANY RESEARCH RESOURCE (Sorry, this position is already filled.)

   If you need more information on a particular topic, consult this person.

Documentation and grading

Team Grade: Each team is responsible for keeping a portfolio. What you include in your portfolio is up to your team members. It should reflect what your group accomplishes on a daily basis; in other words, you should document something every day. (Paychecks and spending ledgers must be included!) Your portfolio will be compared to similar teams from other classes in terms of completed tasks and goals stated above. Your grade will include participation and portfolio work. On-task behavior and participation means you're in character throughout the day.

Class Grade: Soap products will be ranked on quality and quantity with other companies.

REMEMBER: EVERY DECISION, TRANSACTION, AND ACTION SHOULD BE DOCUMENTED AND PLACED IN YOUR PORTFOLIO!

Competition

It should be noted that there are five other companies (classes) about to embark in the same market of selling soap. Therefore, doing your job well is imperative. You want to end up with the "best" product, the product that consumers want and that would make you the most money. (We'll be the judge of what's "best.")

To be honest, both of us chuckle at how meager the early project sheets look, at least in comparison to what we hand out now (shown in Chapter 2). Much time and effort has been put into making the project sheet what it is today. The project objectives have not changed much, but there is much more detailed information concerning project assessment and job descriptions. Of course, these improvements have made the project flow more smoothly, yet the project still requires the students' ingenuity and collaboration to succeed.

The soap project definitely takes the concept of an inquiry-based classroom to a new level. Yes, as the students are immersed in the project, tempers flare, students bicker, and heated discussions occur. Every time we've done this project, we witness true leaders emerge and all the classes are able to get their acts together by the deadline. At some point, students realize that we, as teachers, are not going to step in to solve their problems—it's up to them to do so. And students end up enjoying the challenge. In the first year, 103 out of 106 students said that if given the opportunity, they would do the project again!

We want to reiterate just how frightening it can be to let go of the students' hands and give them the freedom to solve problems on their own, especially with a project with the magnitude of the soap project. In that first year, there were times when we wanted to pull our hair out watching students make mistakes. There were times that a few students were not entirely on task or pulling their weight. There were times that we wanted to scream "freeze" and take over . . . tell them the mistakes they were making. But we kept tight-lipped, recorded what happened throughout the project, and watched each community pull itself together every time. We also talked with each other on a daily basis to assess how the project was going and how we could interject direction through the roles available to us. By doing these things, we maintained our focus of allowing the students to run the classroom.

SEPT	*Scientific Community*
OCT	*Part. Nature of Matter & Gas Laws*
NOV	*Atomic Structure & Per. Trends*
DEC	*Reactions & Stoich.*
JAN	*Stoich.*
FEB	*Equilibrium & Thermo-chemistry*
MAR	*Acids & Bases*
APR	*Organic*
MAY	*Soap* — *Soap Project*
JUNE	*Finals*

2

The Soap Project— Where Are Your Students Headed?

To give you a better sense of how our soap project has evolved over the last ten years, our most recent student soap project handout follows. Then we illustrate how this project plays out in the classroom with another story.

Handout 3—It's Cleanup Time!
(The Soap Project—Latest Revision)

Task

In a cost-effective and creative manner, your company is to produce two pounds of packaged, quality soap that meets and appeals to the consumers' demands of a specified soap market.

Background information

We (the class) are an existing company based in Northbrook, Illinois, that plans to enter the market of producing bar soap for families in the

Northbrook community. Our marketing division in Houston, Texas, has provided us with an initial analysis of the Northbrook community. Assuming that we can take over 20% of the Northbrook "family" market, that each family would purchase seventy-five 140 g-bars per year, and that we stick to a basic recipe of lard, lye, and water, we could make a minimum profit of 10% per bar sold. From our research division in South Charleston, West Virginia, we have obtained an initial small-scale basic recipe that makes ~21 grams of hand soap. This recipe will serve as our foundation for producing the two-pound prototype. Prior to the project, we will become familiar with the process of saponification by using the recipe to make initial soap samples. In addition, a soap expert will inform us of the chemistry behind saponification and take our questions.

Project objectives

1. Improve communication skills.
   - Operate productively and positively in a scientific community.
   - Define a target audience and communicate appropriately to same.
   - Formulate concise, objective-oriented memos.
2. Experience an applicable scientific endeavor.
   - Understand what scientists do and how managers, accountants, and marketers affect what scientists do.
   - Learn one chemical process for producing a desired product.
3. Become familiar with the corporate world.
   - Experience how different teams interact to accomplish a desired goal.
   - Learn how to function under time, monetary, and regulatory constraints.

Project assessment

You are competing against other companies to produce the best soap, best presentation, and best portfolio. See categories below.

Resumé (individual—10 points):

You will be graded on professionalism and content of your resumé. Spend some time on it!

Upper management member or department grade (member/group—30 points):

Each upper management member and each department is responsible for keeping a portfolio which includes but is not limited to: table of contents, goals/time line, daily plans, weekly plans, daily progress reports, weekly progress reports, project summary, paychecks, and copies of memos sent and received. Your portfolio should reflect what you or your group accomplished during the two-week project (project summary) and what you accomplished on a daily basis (daily progress reports). In other words, you should document something every day so that you can write an accurate project summary at the end. Your portfolio will be compared and ranked to like members/groups from other companies in terms of quality in the areas of completed tasks and goals stated above. Please reread your job description so that you'll know the unique materials necessary to include in your portfolio. (Please note: This is a competition against other companies, not your own!) Remember: Every plan, decision, report, transaction, and action should be documented and placed in your portfolio! If you send a note and/or submit a report, keep a copy for yourself! Due by the bell on _____.

Company product grade (class—15 points):

Soap products will be ranked on quality and quantity with other companies. This includes pH, latherability, scent, appearance, consistency (both types), packaging, and cleaning ability. Due by the bell on _____.

Company computer presentation grade (class—15 points):

The class will be presenting on _____ in front of the company representatives. The presentation should use PowerPoint. Remember, you're trying to sell your company. The point of this presentation is to prove that your business and science approaches are the best (cost-effective, meet consumer demands, reproducible large-scale production, your company knows the chemical process of making soap).

Character role-playing grade (individual—30 points):

Your grade will include participation through on-task behavior in the classroom. On-task behavior means you're in character throughout the period from bell to bell, every day. If you're EVER caught doing nothing, or your eyes meet mine, that means you're wasting time and you'll have points deducted. This is a challenge! Rise to the occasion!

Content accountability (individual—20 points):

You will be given a quiz on the chemistry and production of soap on _____. A list of questions outlining the minimum content you should know concerning soap will be handed out.

JOB VACANCIES! APPLY NOW!

Please read the job openings available below. Prepare a resumé by _____ (to be handed in during class) for the position(s) you'd like the most. If you have a first and second choice, please note that on the resumé. Remember, you are competing for these positions. The projected number of positions for each job is indicated next to the job title. Decisions will be based on the content and professionalism of your resumé. Good luck!

Area I: Company departments

RESEARCH SCIENTISTS (8–12):

Using the initial recipe, the research scientists are responsible for planning and performing experiments that will produce the quality of hand soap that meets federal standards, your company's quality program standards, and the public demands of Northbrook community families (obtained through marketing's research). Specifically, the research scientists are responsible for determining how five variables [lard/OH$^-$ ratio, NaOH vs. KOH, reaction temperature, color addition, and scent addition] affect the pH, latherability, scent, appearance, consistency, and cleaning ability of the initial soap recipe product. They are not concerned with the quantity produced (that's the engineers' job) so much as the quality. However, they are expected to assist engineers in doing lab research to help find corrections for any problems that arise during the engineers' final large-scale production of the soap. Because of the slow reaction rate for saponification, the research scientists will be expected to put in overtime in order to maximize lab use. The manager (chosen by the department members) is responsible for preparing daily progress reports for the science supervisor on the group's accomplishments, problems, possible solutions to problems, and adherence to the time line. The manager is also responsible for having his/her group prepare weekly, formal, typed lab reports (due on _____) for the science supervisor that summarize the experimental plans, lab procedures, data (in chart format), data analysis (in appropriate graph format), and conclusions. The research scientists are responsible for submitting chemical and equipment purchase requisitions to the accounting department so that supplies may be obtained from Moon, the company lab assistant. An initial purchase request order is due on the 1st day (_____) of the project (or before), so that you have lab access by day #2. Only those items on the requisition will be given. Those unavailable will be noted. You may not use materials from other departments in the school. Things from home may be used, but only if they meet regulatory standards. All labs *must* take place here!

ENGINEERS (4–6):
Scaling up from the initial recipe, the engineers are responsible for planning and performing experiments that will lead to a better understanding of what process will reproducibly produce the two-pound quantity of hand soap that meets federal standards, your company's quality program standards, and the public demands of Northbrook community families (obtained through marketing's research). Specifically, the engineers are responsible for using stoichiometry to figure out the amounts of each reactant needed, designing a safe lab apparatus, and writing safe lab standard operating procedures and controls that will produce two pounds of hand soap in one batch. They are expected to utilize experimental results gained by the research scientists to correct problems that arise during the large-scale batch production runs. In addition, they are responsible for designing a soap mold that will balance marketing's options of soap shape and withstand the caustic nature of the hydroxide reactant during the saponification reaction.

Because of the slow reaction rate for saponification, the engineers will be expected to put in overtime in order to maximize lab use. The manager is responsible for preparing daily progress reports for the science supervisor on the group's accomplishments, problems, possible solutions to problems, and adherence to the time line. The manager is also responsible for having his/her group prepare weekly, formal, typed lab reports (due on _____) for the science supervisor that summarize the experimental plans, stoichiometric calculations, lab apparatus designs, standard operating procedures/controls, data (in chart format), data analysis (in appropriate graph format), and conclusions. The engineers are responsible for submitting chemical and equipment purchase request orders to the accounting department so that supplies may be obtained from Moon, the company lab assistant. An initial requisition is due on the second day (_____) of the project (or before).

ACCOUNTING (2–3):
The accounting department is responsible for all financial transactions of the company. Specifically, it must prepare a budget statement for the business supervisor's approval which appropriately allocates the $15,000 over the two-week project to the four departments and the upper management team. In preparing this budget statement, it must research average weekly salaries for all positions in the company and determine expected expenses from the department managers. The expected expenses must include but are not limited to lab operations (chemicals, energy use, and equipment), advertising, federal fines, and copying expenses. The initial budget statement is due _____ to the business supervisor. The accountants must develop a computerized program for debits and credits to the company budget so that daily consolidated reports of the company's financial status can be given to the business supervisor. This group is also responsible for processing purchase order requests from the science division for chemicals and equipment that will be obtained from Moon, the company lab assistant. All paychecks are to be written and distributed to each employee on _____. A typed progress report due _____ for the business supervisor will summarize the work of this group over the course of the project.

MARKETING/ADVERTISING/PUBLIC RELATIONS (2–3):

The MAP (Marketing/Advertising/Public Relations) department is responsible for taking a statistically significant hand soap survey, a market/price study on hand soap, and creating an advertising campaign for the company's final product. Specifically, the survey will assess Northbrook community families on their demands for shape, color, and scent of hand soap. The market/price study will consist of an analysis of the range of current soap bar prices available in the community and an analysis of the company's projected profit per bar. The projected profit must take into account the advertising costs in Northbrook, raw materials costs—reactants (see engineers), lab production costs—salaries, equipment, electricity (see accountants), packaging costs, and delivery/shelving costs for at least three key stores in Northbrook. The advertising campaign must include, but is not limited to, product name, slogan, flyer, commercial, web page, advertising through Northbrook's media (3 posters per company, *no* school announcements), and a jingle. The manager is responsible for preparing daily progress reports for the business supervisor on the group's accomplishments, problems, possible solutions to problems, and adherence to the time line. The manager is also responsible for having his/her group prepare a typed progress report due _____ for the business supervisor and science division that summarizes the results of the survey. The second typed progress report due _____ for the business supervisor will summarize the results of the group's market/price study. The advertising campaign will be tested during the second week (5/7–5/17) of the project and documented in the group's portfolio. The advertising campaign must be aligned with the results of the research scientists and engineers. This group must be sure that all aspects of the advertising campaign are submitted to the company lawyer for copyright and trademark approval.

Area II: Upper management team

PLANT MANAGER/VICE PRESIDENT OF COMPANY (1):

The plant manager is in charge of the company, and in turn is responsible for the final production of the soap, company budget, and market analysis and campaign. The vice president will work with the upper management team (prior to the beginning of the project on _____) to develop a detailed time line of daily goals that you think your departments should accomplish throughout the next two weeks. This time line will be given to the department managers on the first day of the project. It is the vice president's overall responsibility to ensure that the company is following this developed time line, making adjustments when necessary. The vice president requests, receives, analyzes, assesses, and reports back on the daily written progress reports received from the business supervisor, science supervisor, and quality control representative. The vice president makes all final decisions on the direction the company will take. These decisions are based on concise, accurate, daily information provided to her/him by the business and science supervisors. The vice president will be in an office working for most of the project. The vice president will prepare weekly progress reports (due on _____) for the company president, Ms. Collins, that summarize the developed time line, the company's accomplishments and adherence to time line, decisions made, problems encountered, and plans for resolution.

SCIENCE SUPERVISOR (1):

The science supervisor is the immediate boss for the managers of the science division: Research Scientists and Engineers. The science supervisor will work with the upper management team (prior to the beginning of the project on _____) to develop a detailed time line of daily goals that you think your departments should accomplish throughout the next two weeks. This time line will be given to the department managers on the first day of the project. The science supervisor works in conjunction with the business supervisor to ensure that both the business and science divisions are working constructively toward accomplishing the goals set out in the developed time line. When adjustments to the time line are necessary, the science supervisor will be responsible for obtaining feedback from the research scientists' and engineers' managers, developing several alternative solutions, and reporting these possible solutions for approval by the vice president. The science supervisor will prepare daily and weekly progress reports (due on _____) for the plant manager that summarize the science division's accomplishments and adherence to time line, decisions made, problems encountered, and plans for problems' resolution.

BUSINESS SUPERVISOR (1):
The business supervisor is the immediate boss for the managers of the business division: Accounting and Marketing/Advertising/Public Relations. She will work with the upper management team (prior to the beginning of the project on _____) to develop a detailed time line of daily goals that you think your departments should accomplish throughout the next two weeks. This time line will be given to the department managers on the first day of the project. The business supervisor works in conjunction with the science supervisor to ensure that both the business and science divisions are working constructively toward accomplishing the goals set out in the developed time line. When adjustments to the time line are necessary, the business supervisor will be responsible for obtaining feedback from the accounting and marketing managers, developing several alternative solutions, and reporting these possible solutions for approval by the plant manager. The business supervisor will prepare daily and weekly progress reports (due on _____) for the vice president that summarize the business division's accomplishments and adherence to time line, decisions made, problems encountered, and plans for problems' resolution.

QUALITY CONTROL SUPERVISOR (1):
The quality control supervisor is responsible for ensuring that the work done by the research scientists and the engineers is quality and passes all standards set by OSHA, the EPA, and the FDA (see the company librarian for a collection of articles). The QC supervisor will work with the upper management team (prior to the beginning of the project on _____) to develop a detailed time line of daily goals that you think the company's departments should accomplish throughout the next two weeks. The QC supervisor is in charge of a documented and publicized quality control program which consists of developing a federal standards training session for

lab employees, a test that each lab employee must pass to ensure that each employee is familiar with written safety and product standards, and a daily "report card" of the company's adherence to the developed quality control program. This program must be in place and made known to lab employees by the first day of the project. Lab employees will not be able to enter the lab area unless you have documentation that they have passed your quality control program test. The QC supervisor is responsible for creating standardized lab tests that the lab employees will use to measure the pH, latherability, scent, appearance, consistency, and cleaning ability of all soap products made in the lab. The QC supervisor is also responsible for acting as lab safety manager, ensuring proper safety accident response and reporting, waste disposal, and lab cleanup procedures. The quality control supervisor will prepare weekly progress reports (due on _____) for the plant manager of the company's adherence to the quality program and be responsible for providing the OSHA representative with the company's "report card" during planned and unplanned inspections of the lab.

OSHA, FDA, AND EPA (ALREADY FILLED—
TO BE ROLE-PLAYED BY THE TEACHER):
The Occupational Safety and Health Administration, the Food and Drug Administration, and the Environmental Protection Agency are the monkey wrenches in your plan! These three agencies have outlined standards with which you must comply on a daily basis. Failing to do so results in fines and possible company shutdown. Compliance checklists will be written if fines are imposed. (QC should do research to find out what these standards are. See job description.)

COMPANY LIBRARIAN (ALREADY FILLED—
TO BE ROLE-PLAYED BY THE SCHOOL LIBRARIAN):
The company librarian, Ms. Sue Eddington, will help you obtain resources concerning soap production, federal standards, salaries, and Northbrook community information. She currently has a collection of articles and books on these topics in the library. Should you need further assistance, make an appointment to go see her.

COMPANY LAWYER (ALREADY FILLED—
TO BE ROLE-PLAYED BY THE TEACHER):
The company lawyer, Ms. Reywal, is responsible for copyrighting all information given to her on the company's behalf. The name of the company, the name of the soap, and any slogans need licenses. Borrowed slogans, etc. need permission. Trademarks for logos, etc. need licenses.

COMPANY TECHNOLOGY SPECIALIST (ALREADY FILLED—
TO BE FILLED BY A SCHOOL TECHNOLOGY EMPLOYEE):
Mr. Todd Huettel will help you with any technology-based questions. These questions might pertain to the use of the mobile lab during class and/or to the presentation you'll be using for the representatives.

COMPANY PRESIDENT (ALREADY FILLED—
TO BE ROLE-PLAYED BY THE TEACHER):
Ms. Collins will be here periodically. Be prepared!
  Keep this sheet! Use it as a reference *throughout* the project!

In character as company president, the teacher says to her "employees" (students), "Congratulations on your new jobs. Your objective is to produce two pounds of quality, packaged soap. I trust your company will have a prototype when I return in two weeks. I now leave you in the very capable hands of your vice president." She points to a student. She leaves the room and doesn't speak to her "employees" until the end of the project.

Wearing a name tag that says, "I'm a figment of your imagination," the teacher sits in the corner of the classroom frantically typing on the computer. She's observing and recording everything heard in the room. She's a shadow. The students cannot speak to her. On this first day of the project, she observes that the class is working on accomplishing the seemingly simple task mentioned above. They have broken up into their respective departments. There are twelve research scientists and five chemical engineers in the lab working on soap samples and experiments. Three marketing/advertising personnel are brainstorming company names and two accountants are researching average salaries for all employees. The three supervisors and vice president are walking around the room, making sure that these objectives are met.

On the fifth day of the project, she overhears the following conversation between the company supervisors. "Tomorrow I think we should focus our attention on testing the different scents. According to marketing, our surveys concluded that families want a rose-scented soap," the Business Supervisor says. With conviction the Science Supervisor responds, "We can't test the scents until we have a good first sample of soap! My research scientists need one more day before that can happen." The Vice President concurs, "OK, one more day for initial samples. Then we figure out how to add the scent. Let's send a memo with the amended agenda to all departments." The Quality Control Supervisor disappears in order to find the MSDS information on the rose scent.

On the seventh day, her students are starting to feel the reality of a deadline approaching. "Hey, you guys, the research scientists wrote us a memo saying that they can't figure out how to make the soap safe enough to handle without gloves! It's too corrosive." The marketing department chuckles. "So I guess we'll have to rethink our packaging materials so that the soap doesn't eat through it on the store shelves." More laughs.

The accounting manager shouts over to the business supervisor, "I think the engineers did their stoichiometry incorrectly. Why the heck should we spend $28.99 on 500 g of NaOH? They only need 212 g!" Another accountant is frantically trying to print out all the company paychecks before the end of company time. Today is payday.

The engineers are working on making a mold for the soap. "How does this design look?" They all huddle together and look at a sketch on a piece of paper. One engineer asks, "Now what material should we use to build it so that these chemicals don't eat through it?" One engineer quips, "Shouldn't we already know this? Shouldn't we already have a mold?" Another responds sarcastically and with a bit of desperation, "Of course we should! And we should be in the lab making the two pounds of soap already, but we're not. So let's focus on one thing at a time, shall we?" There's a moment of silence, then the engineering manager starts panicking and delegating one job after another to every member of the department.

And the largest group (the research scientists) is in the back of the room working in the lab area. They are all wearing pants, closed-toed shoes, long sleeves, gloves, and goggles. The scientists are measuring, mixing, documenting, and observing in order to determine the final recipe for the engineers.

On the last day of the project, the teacher observes a bustle of activity. By the end of class time, students must turn in two pounds of quality, packaged soap, along with eight portfolios, one for each department, documenting everything they did over the last two weeks. One student nervously watches the clock tick down the last thirty seconds of the project. One department still has some stray sheets to put in its accounting portfolio. But sure enough, at the twelve-second mark, Accounting throws its completed portfolio on the front lab table with the other seven. The company breathes a collective sigh of relief and then bursts out in applause. "We did it!"

And they did. They did the whole thing on their own. They achieved their goals by doing phenomenal things in their self-directed scientific community. They had the freedom to explore on their own and discover what they were capable of achieving. The term "self-sufficient scientific community" means something to them now, not just the teacher.

The soap project, shown by Handout 3—IT'S CLEANUP TIME! (The Soap Project), is our culminating, end-of-the-year activity. It details what our classroom looks and sounds like at the end of the school year. It is our goal to get our students prepared for an undertaking like this one. They are obviously not ready for something of this nature at the beginning of the year. We wanted to give the reader a picture of an actual self-sufficient scientific community in action as a starting point. The focus throughout our book is how to create this classroom. Although we know the reader may be skeptical as to the truth of this story, we hope to allay some disbelief as we share our experiences.

We realize that there are many reasons why a teacher would not want to do a project like this one. (We address many of these in Chapter 3.) For a teacher who cares, the most haunting reason is that you don't want your students to struggle. It's an incredibly draining experience. It's like letting go of a toddler's hand when she's learning to walk. She walks sometimes and falls sometimes. But she has to figure it out for herself. You can only carry her so long. As a parent, you've got to give her the struggle, even though you'd much rather do the guiding. As teachers, we feel the same way. This project allows students to "walk" sometimes and "fall" sometimes. But they figure it out for themselves. That's why the project is so successful, meaningful, and authentic. They own it.

Here's what some of the students included in their project evaluations, located in their previously mentioned portfolios:

1. "I like the idea of us being blindfolded and dropped in the middle of nowhere and then being asked to find our own way home using only each other as resources."
2. "I learned so much about myself. Some good. Some scary."
3. "I loved this project. It was fun to see our progress without the help of a teacher."
4. "I totally loved this project. I got so much out of it and walked away with a new knowledge of my strengths and weaknesses. I think this is because I was having to really think without asking the teacher."
5. "I really enjoyed doing this project. It was the ultimate test to see if we could learn and work on our own. Nobody's ever given me that opportunity before. I didn't even know what I was capable of. Thanks!"

We know how to create the innovative classroom above. We've done it year after year. In this book we will tell a story of how to shift the balance of who's running the classroom from teacher to student. This shift in balance is what makes the rather dry idea of the constructivist theory come to life in our classrooms. Though many books explain what the theory is, they don't provide a holistic and practical example of how to implement it throughout an entire school year. Instead, these methodology books describe a series of unrelated activities. Our approach is to share how we implement this theory from September to June and end up with a self-sufficient scientific community of learners who care.

This activity, the soap project, is the one we use to test whether or not we've accomplished our shift appropriately, whether or not we've helped to create a self-sufficient scientific community. And every year, we are amazed by each class that becomes this ideal vision of a classroom truly run by students. That's where we're headed . . .

SEPT	*Scientific Community*
OCT	*Part. Nature of Matter & Gas Laws*
NOV	*Atomic Structure & Per. Trends*
DEC	*Reactions & Stoich.*
JAN	*Stoich.*
FEB	*Equilibrium & Thermo-chemistry*
MAR	*Acids & Bases*
APR	*Organic*
MAY	*Soap*
JUNE	*Finals*

This Style of Teaching Incorporated All Year Long

3

Can This Style of Teaching Work?

"In your dreams! There's no way your class worked for two weeks without a teacher's direction. That could *never* happen!"

We imagine a good number of readers—like some of our coworkers have been in the past—are quite skeptical about the soap activity described in Chapters 1 and 2. First of all, yes, it really can happen. And second, yes, we know you have a number of logistical questions about how we get our classroom functioning in this manner.

Getting the students to work as constructively and efficiently as described in Chapter 2 takes us an entire school year. A given class requires eight months of practice to gain the content and skills necessary to successfully complete a project like "soap." But it can be done, with any class from any high school. To alleviate some of your anxiety, we'd like to address some of the most frequently asked questions from teachers who wonder how we can give a class so much freedom without allowing chaos to run rampant.

1. *How did you develop your inquiry-based teaching styles? Why do you teach like this?*

Our teaching styles (Joan's and Dennis') are quite similar and are rooted in many unique life experiences. The most significant contributing factor that formed our inquiry-based approach to teaching science is simply that we remember how much fun it was as children to ask questions and explore. We've always loved science. We still find our environment fascinating and have maintained the ability to continually question the "how" and "why." It made sense to us to try to rekindle the same inherent curiosity in our students in order for them to have as much fun with science as we do. We share some stories in the beginning of Chapter 4 that will elaborate on this; in short, we want our enthusiasm and fascination for the mysteries of science to be contagious. So we do what we can to get our students hooked.

2. *What benefit is there to teaching this way as opposed to using a traditional approach in the science classroom? In other words, how do you align your teaching style with the standards?*

First of all, we don't want to mislead anyone. We still use traditional teaching methods in our classroom. We lecture, do demos, assign homework including textbook reading, give tests, and do lab activities. However, we do try to limit lessons that only disseminate information or require students to regurgitate facts during the entire period. Instead, we use these traditional methods to supplement our more frequent inquiry-based lessons. Our goal is to get the students excited about doing science by, simply put, letting them do science! *Doing* science allows students to formulate good questions, design and perform true experiments, think critically about the outcome, draw an educated conclusion as to "how" and "why" something happened, and appropriately communicate these findings to a wide range of target audiences. These skills then lend themselves to every arena outside the science classroom.

Coincidentally, the majority of our lessons align themselves with the standards given in the *National Science Education Standards*, published in 1996. Specifically, our approach to teaching aligns itself with the teaching standards A–F, as follows:

Teaching Standard A: Teachers of science plan an inquiry-based science program for their students.

Teaching Standard B: Teachers of science guide and facilitate learning.

Teaching Standard C: Teachers of science engage in ongoing assessment of their teaching and of student learning.

Teaching Standard D: Teachers of science design and manage learning environments that provide students with the time, space, and resources needed for learning science.

Teaching Standard E: Teachers of science develop communities of science learners that reflect the intellectual rigor of scientific inquiry and the attitudes and social values conducive to science learning.

Teaching Standard F: Teachers of science actively participate in the ongoing planning and development of the school science program.

The benefit of using the inquiry-based method of teaching science is clearly laid out in the follow-up document, *Inquiry and the National Science Education Standards* (2000). Our lessons are also impressively aligned with this additional call to incorporate inquiry-based teaching into science education programs. The council states that the research done on inquiry-based teaching "clearly suggests that teaching through inquiry is effective" (p. 126). The council further describes individual studies that were directed at special student populations around the world, showing: "A pattern of general support for inquiry-based teaching continues to emerge from the research." A university-level study (also mentioned on page 126), which we believe to be particularly interesting, found that regardless of scores, students learning through inquiry have a higher motivation to do science (Heywood and Heywood 1992).

3. *Do the students run the classroom right at the beginning of the year? Do you step back and put them in charge in September?*

Absolutely not. We take many factors into consideration when deciding how to get our students ready to function as a self-sufficient scientific community. No class would be successful being completely on its own at the beginning of the year. We guide our students through the steps necessary to function effectively without us. Some classes pick up on these skills more quickly than others through the first few months. The level of students, the type of class, the personality and maturity of the students all play a role in the amount of freedom we're willing to offer at a particular point in the year.

At the start of the year, we give the class smaller projects and/or labs that take one to three days to complete. Specific examples of these activities are explained in Chapters 4 and 5 of the book. We help them establish a class climate that nurtures a community approach to solving problems. We guide them through projects by answering questions, facilitating discussions, suggesting problem-solving methods, and role-playing different characters that will help them accomplish a task. Once they have a solid foundation of the minimum that is expected, individually and as a class, we slowly remove ourselves from the equation. Rest assured, before turning them loose in a culminating end-of-the-year activity, we take it slowly, introducing them to all the skills and content necessary to succeed without the aid of a teacher.

4. *How do you get all the content in when you give the students so much time to "discover"?*

The *National Science Education Standards* includes the content standards A–G, as follows:

Content Standard A: Science as Inquiry
Content Standard B: Physical Science
Content Standard C: Life Science
Content Standard D: Earth and Space Science
Content Standard E: Science and Technology
Content Standard F: Science in Personal and Social Perspective
Content Standard G: History and Nature of Science

Our book provides an approach to teaching that squarely hits on content standards A and B. Some of our activities also briefly cover E, F, and G. These activities could easily be adapted for whatever content area needs to be covered in other science classes, like those mentioned in content standards C and D.

Giving students time to discover does not always mean sacrificing content. As we've stated, we still have days where we lecture, do demonstrations, and run lab activities that are more teacher-directed. So we find ourselves still getting through the majority of the content outlined within a particular curriculum. However, we typically have an inquiry-based "twist" whenever we're giving a lecture or performing a demo, to keep the students thinking. For instance, when introducing the mole, we do not begin a lecture by defining the mole and spending a half hour explaining it to the students. Rather, we think of a focus question to get the students interested. For example, "There's a liter of water in this glass. Before I drink it, how many molecules of water do you think are in it?" We write their ideas on the board and hold a discussion on which answers seem reasonable. Students are asked to justify what "reasonable" means. Then we give a ten-minute lecture on the concept of the mole. Later we go back to the glass of water and challenge the students to answer the initial question. As a follow-up, more demos are introduced with probing questions, and homework practice problems are assigned. In this way, we get through the content using a variety of methods as the students develop a deeper understanding of the mole.

However, it is true that we sometimes must sacrifice one unit in order to allow the students to investigate another topic in depth. As teachers, it's been tough to let go of some of the content and decide which topics to cover and which to cut. No matter what teaching methods you use, there never seems to be enough time. However, research suggests that "this 'cover everything' approach provides few opportunities for students to acquire anything but surface knowledge on any topic" (Schmidt et al. 1997). Our focus is not only to get students to a point where they can act as scientists, but to also enjoy doing so at the same time. Teaching them an inordinate number of meaningless science facts does not accomplish this. But having them delve deeper into a unit gives them this opportunity. Less is more!

5. *What about the student who might be unwilling to actively participate in a class project once you've "handed over the reins"?*

Most often, these unwilling students are more likely to participate when their peers are in charge. We have found that the class is sometimes more effective at creating an atmosphere where this type of student will want to participate. For example, Dennis had a disruptive student who tried his patience during teacher-led activities. However, when the student's peers were in charge, he would become quite cooperative and congenial. The students were familiar with his behavior from previous years and knew better how to work with him.

Sometimes a student still remains unwilling to participate even with peers in charge. But this happens either way; with or without the teacher, this student is not going to do much of anything. And everyone recognizes that. The community learns to pick up the slack and get the job done. Think of a class with twenty-six students. In a student-led project with a nonparticipating student, the teacher is certain that twenty-five out of twenty-six students are actively involved. In a teacher-led lesson, the teacher would have proof concerning only the one nonparticipatory student. It's still uncertain whether the other twenty-five are actually involved with what you are teaching. So this represents a huge advantage in using inquiry-based, student-led activities.

6. *I'm still hesitant. When you say you're going to hand the class over to the students, I'm always concerned with time on task. Regardless of the length of a project—one day, three days, ten days—what internal motivation are your students using for the majority of the class to stay on task? Without prompting from me throughout a period, it seems surreal that they would actually stick to it. How do you get this to work?*

It's not as difficult as you might think. We describe the beginning steps to this process in detail in Chapter 4. But simply put, if you trust them to do something and they know you believe that they can, and if you present the activity in an enthusiastic manner, they will typically respond by living up to your expectations. We were hesitant, too, the first time we "let go" and left them in charge. But we realized after the first activity we tried, students are desperate for this opportunity. They're tired of being spoon-fed, even if they don't realize it at first. We didn't know what would happen because we had never tried it before and had never heard of anyone else trying it before. But after going through a couple years of letting our students *do science*, students at every level, we did not see chaos erupt, as most teachers predict. Instead, we saw students getting excited about science again, about being given the opportunity to control a bit of their own education.

There are certainly things you must do as a teacher to steer a class in the right direction at the beginning of the year to get students used to this new method of learning. One class may need nothing from you. This class takes on a personality that loves a challenge and will fly with any task you put in front of them. Another class may need some prompting questions or pictures drawn or charades to be played to get them on the right track. And still another class might need you to direct quite a few activities until they get the hang of it. After all these years of using this inquiry-based approach in our classrooms, we still experiment with what works for each unique class.

Another key ingredient in getting our students to build a scientific community and to stay on task while working as a class is for us to stay focused on preparing them for the final project. These are not isolated activities that we introduce to our classes. Every day they experience some individual and class accountability. They know it isn't going away, so they learn to work within the system we set up.

7. *How do you grade a class project?*

It's tough to answer this question with a blanket rubric for all class activities. Each project is unique. We did outline how the soap project is graded on the actual project sheet, Handout 3. It contains both individual and class grades. In general, we want to teach our students to develop an appreciation for the fact that both group and individual accountability is important. To be an effective member of a class/company, you must first be as prepared as possible individually. In terms of encouraging individual preparation, we use traditional methods of assessment to see how well students are keeping up—quizzes, homework, tests, etc.

Although each project is unique, the grading of the class work is typically split into three categories:

A. The first is safety. During a class quiz, class lab, class project, or class test (examples described in detail in Chapter 5), the class is given credit for how well they follow safety procedures. This includes obtaining MSDS information on all chemicals involved, using proper lab technique, policing each other to make sure everyone is safe, having equipment ready in case of an accident (like baking soda for an acid spill), and proper cleanup of lab.

B. The second category is accuracy. We check the work that is turned in, just as we would an individual test, quiz, or lab, to make sure the responses are correct.

C. The third category is cooperation. We look for positive conversations, a constructive group effort, on-task behavior, and a high level of group intensity to get the challenges finished.

As an example of points given for these three categories, in a class test worth 12 points, each area (A, B, and C) is given equal weight of 4 points. Every student in the class would then receive the same number of points out of 12, since it was a class test.

In general, assessing an inquiry-based classroom and the activities that go along with it takes some practice. The *National Science Education Standards* list five areas to focus on:

Assessment Standard A: Assessments must be consistent with the decisions they are designed to inform.
Assessment Standard B: Achievement and the opportunity to learn science must be assessed.
Assessment Standard C: The technical quality of the data collected is well matched to the decisions and actions taken on the basis of their interpretation.
Assessment Standard D: Assessment practices must be fair.
Assessment Standard E: The inferences made from assessments about student achievement and opportunity to learn must be sound.

Reading these standards can be quite confusing and frankly very frustrating to follow. In our opinion, the best approach is to give the students feedback on all parts of their experiences in your class—from individual, content-focused tests to the journey a community takes while solving a problem. In this way the assessment will give both the teacher and the students information on where to go next in developing their scientific community.

8. *What has been the parental response to the idea of inquiry-based group work? How do they feel about group grades?*

    As far as parental response to our group activities, it has been overwhelmingly supportive. Most parents understand that industry is based on collaborative work. They, like us, feel that individual accountability is still very important, but that students need to practice working toward common goals as a group. Together, we've had hundreds of parent letters and phone calls from all different districts praising the methods we use in our classroom.

    The parents who are "concerned" about our group activities seem to call only regarding the grades their children receive that are group oriented. Combined, we have received a total of nine negative phone calls in reference to group grades. Over fourteen years and between two teachers, that's not bad. It's interesting to note that for all nine cases, the parents rescinded their concern when they learned that their child's grade went down after removing the group grades from their child's points. So this, in our minds, should not be a major concern as a teacher.

9. *What happens when I implement the activities described in this book and the goals are not achieved?*

    The intention of this book is to provide you with the curricular foundation in implementing a constructivist approach into the science classroom. Certainly adjustments must be made to all activities presented here depending on the level of students, the personality of the classroom community, the response of unique classes to these activities, and the content or unit being covered. These adjustments are not discussed in this book. These are the details added to lesson plans by individual teachers. Adjustments are also best implemented using classroom management skills and teaching strategies that individual teachers deem best based on their own personality and teaching style. So we leave the job of making these lessons come alive to you.

A good number of readers may still have reservations, but we hope we have addressed some of the more common, immediate hesitations. Now we would like to describe how we begin setting up our scientific community, which is the focus of our next chapter.

	Scientific Community	Where Do You Start?
SEPT		
OCT	*Part. Nature of Matter & Gas Laws*	
NOV	*Atomic Structure & Per. Trends*	
DEC	*Reactions & Stoich.*	
JAN	*Stoich.*	
FEB	*Equilibrium & Thermo-chemistry*	
MAR	*Acids & Bases*	
APR	*Organic*	
MAY	*Soap*	
JUNE	*Finals*	

4

Where Do You Start?

It's the start of a new school year. You are greeting students at the door of your room on the first day. Approximately half of your new class has arrived. You then notice that the students are milling around the room and you are dismayed that you haven't thought of where they should sit; you haven't even made a seating chart yet. Once all of them arrive, the bell rings and you proceed to the front of the room. Much to your surprise and shock, the students are walking around the room, chatting with friends about vacations, summer parties, and life in general. They are paying no attention to you. You decide to get their attention by starting with your first planned activity, but astounded, you realize you have no lesson plan and you haven't the foggiest idea why you don't have a lesson plan. The class gets noisier and more chaotic, making you completely anxious about what the coming year has in store for you. Some students start yelling at each other. You go over to alleviate the situation. Meanwhile, you notice a few students walking out of the room. Others are dancing to music. You can't believe what's happening! Then with a gasp and sweat running down your face, you wake up and realize thankfully that you were only dreaming . . .

All teachers go through some type of anxiety before a new school year. We do every year. It is normal to want to start the school year out on the right foot, grabbing and maintaining the attention of the students, and continuing to explore the infinite mysteries in science for the remainder of the year. We have found that the place to start is by helping the students develop their classroom scientific community. Starting on the first day, we create a model scientific community in our classrooms and continue to facilitate this climate by incorporating unique activities throughout the year. During our first week of school, we focus on the five important aspects involved in building our classroom communities so that they will function successfully, with or without our guidance, by the end of the year. The foundation of a self-sufficient scientific community is rooted in climate, trust, journals (record-keeping), safety, and cooperation. We realized that these were a necessary beginning to building our communities mainly through experience, but also through interviewing more than one hundred different industry-based companies, asking them what they would do to improve their workplace. So, the first five days of school are focused on giving our students the opportunity to experience what these mean and to illustrate that they are a necessary part of our classroom.

Climate

SEPT	*Scientific Community*	*Climate*

"Close your eyes. Tell me what vision *first* pops into your head when you hear the following." Ms. Gallagher asks, "What do you picture when you hear the word *scientist*?"

The students are quiet for a minute. They slowly open their eyes, most having a grin on their face from what they just pictured. Ms. Gallagher says, "OK, let me hear it. What did you see?"

Erica responds, "A lab coat, messy hair, goggles, test tubes, beakers."

Other students share their ideas.

"Einstein!"

"Definitely a man."

"Mr. Johnston!" (The whole class is in agreement. This was their science teacher from last year.)

They continue. "Someone writing things down in a book."

"Explosions."

"A guy with a pocket protector."

"Bad clothes."

"A guy working on a computer."

"Someone making observations."

Ms. Gallagher classifies their responses on the board into two categories: actions and objects.

Then she asks, "What do you picture when you think of this same scientist in a building with other scientists? What has changed? Anything?"

"They're arguing."

"Emailing to each other."

"Presenting information to one another, like in a dark room with an overhead and a laser pointer in a monotone voice." The class chuckles.

"They're using fax machines to send their findings to other places."

"Deciding what to do next."

"Talking in 'science lingo.'"

"They're on the phone ordering material."

A pause. Ms. Gallagher asks, "So what's the big difference between the scientist who was alone and the group of scientists?"

"The same stuff as before; you just have people talking to one another."

By guiding the students through this conversation, we help our students to discover that the main difference between the two scenarios is communication. Our students are told that in this science classroom, they will *not* be working alone during their science investigations. Rather, they will be working as a community of scientists. This is our goal for this lesson.

Ms. Gallagher continues, "Your image of a scientist is too narrow-minded. It's obvious that you're thinking that a scientist is a white male in a lab coat with glasses or goggles and a pocket protector. He is working alone or in a group of similar white males, and solving the world's problems. Come on!" The class laughs. "Think again! All of you have behaved like scientists in the past. Let me give you an example that might jog your memory and open your mind."

"When my oldest daughter was two years old, I used to drop her off at a friend's house on my way to work. She always carried her 'blankie' with her. One morning, she sat up and screamed that her blankie was changing colors. She asked me why. Then, the car stopped and she said, 'Oh, never mind, Mom. It's OK now.' Once the car started moving again, she sat up and screamed that her blankie was changing colors again. 'Mommy, why is it changing colors? Make it stop!' She threw it at me and started to cry. I pulled over and reassured her that everything was OK. Again, she looked at the blanket and said, 'Never mind. It's OK again.' The third time it happened, I realized what was going on. I reassured her not to be afraid. And I asked her, 'Katina, what do you think is making your blankie change colors?' For about two weeks, she was fascinated by this problem. One day she noticed the shadow of her hand on the blanket. She moved her hand back and forth and noticed that the blankie didn't change colors in the shadow of her hand. This discovery occupied her thoughts for another two weeks. Finally, one morning she decided to look out the window. She noticed that it was the shadows caused by the streetlights that made her blankie 'change colors.' It was as if the world was lifted from her shoulders. She had made an amazing discovery. She had done so with prompting from me and her own determination.

Mr. Smithenry tells another story to his class, "When I was five or six, I remember sitting alone in our living room watching the sunlight stream in through the curtains. I saw small particles floating around. I thought that I had seen air. I ran and got my older sister to look at my discovery. She told me that it was dust. I wasn't convinced so I asked my mom. She confirmed my sister's response and explained that the dust settled on the surfaces in the room, thus making it necessary to dust the furniture. The question was settled for the time being; however, I sat again and observed further. The dust particles were moving up and down and didn't seem to settle. I also wondered where these dust particles came from. Where was their continual source if they were settling? Over a decade later in chemistry class my question was answered with the kinetic theory, at least for the time being . . ." Again, his story illustrated brainstorming between people and his own inquisitiveness.

Ms. Gallagher shares another story with her class. "My younger daughter loves forts and building things. Once, when she was about four, she was building this elaborate fort in the family room out of pillows, couches, tables, and blankets. Eventually she came running into the kitchen and asked me, "Mom, why won't this stay up?" She handed me a pillow. "This is supposed to be one of the walls of my fort and it keeps falling down! I've tried it all different ways." So I took her into the family room and said, "I think I see the problem, Kira. You tell me, how is this pillow different from the other pillows that are being used for walls?" It only took her a moment, she looked up at me with a smile and said, "I got it. Thanks, Mom." I watched her rearrange the fort, using the largest pillows for the sides and the smallest pillows for anchors. She, too, had figured out her problem through observation, prompting, and determination.

To our students, we then say, "Now think for a moment of examples where you were working with other people—like when Katina and Kira worked with their mom or when Mr. Smithenry worked with his sister and mom—maybe performing some of the actions on our 'action' list, using some of the objects on our 'object' list, in order to solve a problem."

In the preceding dialog, you'll notice that the teacher is directing the conversation. The teacher is in charge. She or he is guiding the students in order to make the connection between their stories and how we are going to operate in this classroom. We are starting the classroom off by building their self-esteem, reminding them that they can do science. This teacher-led discussion reinforces behaviors that students have been engaged in all their lives while discovering the world around them. The three main points of this activity are that the students revisit that they behave as scientists, that they remember that it is instinctively worthwhile for them to act as a community, and that they reconnect with their inherent curiosity.

Virginia hesitantly raises her hand and says, "I don't know if this is what you mean, but when I was on the beach this summer, I saw some stuff in the water that glowed. I asked my dad about it. He and I then looked it up together on Grolier's. It was fun!"

"Yes! That's exactly what I mean," the teacher reassures Virginia. "You worked together with your dad to investigate a problem."

Eric's memory was jogged. He raises his hand excitedly and says, "Yeah, when I was little, I had this clown. If you punched it, it fell down and would always pop back up. I asked my brother why it did that. He said there was sand in the bottom. I didn't believe him, so I cut it open!" The class laughed. "He was right!"

The students begin to feel more comfortable opening up in front of each other, sharing their personal experiences. The students then have an immediate feel for what the classroom atmosphere will be like for the remainder of the year. They realize that the climate in which they will experience this year of science is one that emphasizes and nurtures a community effort, that everyone has something worthwhile to offer the class. By being active members on the first day of school, they've taken their first steps at creating a scientific community.

The follow-up to this first day's activity, which is described in the next section, "Trust," is crucial to maintaining this type of environment.

Trust

SEPT	Scientific Community	Trust

"Hello, class. My name is Ms. Solob. I'm your substitute teacher for today. I have some tragic news to share with you. Ms. Gallagher, your new chemistry teacher, died last night. I know what she was planning to do today, so I've created a slightly different lesson plan to cover the same material. One of her colleagues stopped by her house and gathered a few artifacts for our lesson. Let's break up into six groups. Each group take a box of artifacts belonging to the late Ms. Gallagher. Write down ten statements you believe to be true about her. We'll reconvene after ten minutes.

After our students are introduced to the "scientific community" climate, we work on trust. We believe that it is imperative for our students to trust us if we wish to get them to commit to the idea of working together. The best way to develop trust is to first trust them. We do this by allowing them to accomplish a task as a community of students without the "teacher" on the second day. Instead of the teacher, we role-play as a substitute teacher. We dress slightly differently, coming in costume, and enter class introducing ourselves as a substitute. This "sub" has brought in some personal possessions of the "late teacher" (us) and wants the class to help write an obituary/biography based on these artifacts. (See Handout 4—The Death of Ms. Gallagher.) There are several important reasons for doing such an unorthodox activity on the second day:

- It allows the students to act as a community to scientifically analyze the teacher.
- It shows you trust them to act responsibly with your personal possessions.

- It allows you to effectively sneak in such things as collaborative assignments and roles, discussion skills, and classroom rules without them feeling the "teacher" is doing it.
- It allows you to teach the difference between observations and interpretations.
- And most importantly, it is preparing the students for future student-directed class assignments.

Students working in their groups look eagerly at Ms. Gallagher's personal artifacts. They're excited to be finding out about their teacher.

"What's this thing?" a student asks, holding up a *matryoshka* doll.

Another group says, "Look! Ms. Gallagher got in a car accident. She must be a terrible driver."

A third group is writing frantically: "Gosh, we know a lot about Ms. Gallagher now! How many statements should we write again?"

After ten minutes, Ms. Solob—the disguised Ms. Gallagher—then asks each group manager, "What are the two most interesting statements that your group came up with?" She writes their responses on the board for all to see. Some responses included,

"Ms. Gallagher liked alternative music."
"Ms. Gallagher has a son and a daughter."
"No, she has two daughters!"
"Ms. Gallagher traveled a lot."
"She was really smart."
"She lived in Russia at some point."

Ms. Solob then tells the groups, "Trade boxes with another group and see if you would modify any of the statements written in your journals, or those we wrote on the board. Take five minutes to look at this new box. Then we'll reconvene again."

After the "substitute" teacher gets all the statements and modifications written on the board, she says to the class, "Before addressing the statements on the board, let's define the terms *observation* and *interpretation*." Ms. Solob writes the definitions on the board and then asks, "Going back to our statements about Ms. Gallagher, which of them are observations and which are interpretations?"

Throughout the activity, the class discussion is led by the "substitute." The students then volunteer to classify the statements on the board as observations or interpretations. In the end, they realize that all (or most) are interpretations. Later on in the week during our first lab, we refer back to this lesson and remind them about observations and interpretations. While in lab, students record observations. Afterwards, they should spend time brainstorming together on interpreting these observations.

Certainly our students have had science before, and have therefore discussed observations and interpretations. But when preparing them to work in groups, we want to make sure that everyone is on the same page. And we're always surprised at how easily these two are confused, even by students sixteen and seventeen years old. So we set the record straight. However, this is only the content portion of today's activity. The trust issue is the major objective. And we subtly weave it into a content-based lesson.

> "We haven't even addressed whether or not we think these statements are true," Ms. Solob says. "How many of you are confident that 50 percent or more of these statements are true?" A majority of the class raises hands. "Wow! OK, so how many of you think that 75 percent or more of these statements are true?" Quite a few hands drop. "Oh, not so confident anymore, are we? And how many of you think that 100 percent of what's written on the board was true about Ms. Gallagher?" No hands remain raised. Finally, Ms. Solob asks, "Well what could you do to increase your confidence with the number of truths we know about Ms. Gallagher?"
>
> A brief silence fills the room. Finally, Jane's eyes brighten. She raises her hand and says, "Well, what if we were given time to look at all the boxes with all the groups? Couldn't we then better determine what made sense about Ms. Gallagher?"

We spend some time talking with the class about the realization Jane just made. The students conclude that the activity they just did represents the scientific community we discussed yesterday. They also find that a true scientific community will never be able to absolutely verify that it has the right answer. Scientists can only make conclusions based on the data in front of them. The more data they share, the more likely it is that they're approaching the "right" answer. And with more accurate information, ideally scientists are better able to suggest constructive paths to solving problems.

And your lesson is now complete. You reached the two most important goals. The students see the benefit in working as a community. "Two minds are better than one." And they realize that they came to a conclusion as a group with no help from Ms. Gallagher, and very little help from the "substitute" teacher. They've taken their first step closer to running the scientific community "on their own."

Handout 4—The Death of Ms. Gallagher

An exercise in observation vs. interpretation using artifacts

(This activity has been modified from the original activity created by Mr. Spiro Bolos.)

> *Scene 1:* Upon arriving at school today, you are shocked and saddened to discover that Ms. Gallagher, your mysterious chemistry teacher, has kicked the proverbial bucket.
>
> *Scene 2:* At first, you think, "Although I am very sad at the passing of Ms. Gallagher, I am relieved that I won't have any chemistry homework for the rest of the year!"
>
> *Scene 3:* Wrong. You are surprised by the appearance of Ms. Solob, who has been hired as your substitute teacher for the day.
>
> *Scene 4:* Ms. Solob produces a small box filled with personal belongings (or "artifacts") from the late Ms. Gallagher. "Your assignment," she smiles, "is to get to know Ms. Gallagher as best you can based on what you may find in your box."

Discoveries

Working with the other members in your group, write down 10 statements in your journal that you believe to be true about Ms. Gallagher based on the materials in the box. Give a brief reason for your statements.

Observation vs. interpretation

From her belongings, what did you observe and what did you interpret? (Use the board!)

Questions

1. What is an artifact? (You may have heard this in a history class.)
2. Define *observation*. What is a qualitative observation? A quantitative observation?
3. Define *interpretation*.

Goals

- "Two" minds are better than one.
- You should leave this class in June with more *questions* than answers!
- You are, always have been, and always will be a scientist. You don't need a teacher to behave that way.

Death of Ms. Gallagher teacher info

Items to include in the boxes that are handed out for this activity vary widely. We've put pictures, receipts, tools, toys, books, concert tickets, kitchen utensils, keys, transcripts, etc. Anything random from around the house works. It doesn't have to have any significance; after all, most of us have random junk everywhere!

Journals

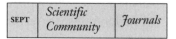

Ms. Gallagher puts a transparency on the overhead and the students study the image. She asks them, "What do you see?" They respond that they see sketches, labels, writings, lines, and other information that's illegible.

"This is a page from Leonardo da Vinci's journal. He was the king of journaling. I know it doesn't appear that way. This page looks illegible, but there's a reason for that. It's old! And it's written in mirror image writing." She describes for them what that means. She then continues, "In terms of the content, however, I want you to work on keeping a journal as detailed as da Vinci's throughout this year. That means, at a minimum, your journal should function as the following: it is a calendar, a notebook, a sketch pad, a diary, and a book for documenting lab information. In other words, you are writing a book about your experiences in this class from Day 1 to Day 182."

We then explain to the students that they should purchase a composition-type notebook to serve as their journal. This is our personal preference, but we like the students to get a realistic feel for behaving as scientists. The majority of research and industry labs use a hardbound book for keeping records. We also do this because it's easier on us when we collect them. Spiral notebooks can wreak havoc on clothing and car interiors.

We cannot emphasize enough the importance of students keeping journals. Keeping all the content organized throughout the year is beneficial for them so they know where everything is. And as the year progresses, the students can picture how our units come together to create a story about chemistry. The definition of the word *chemistry* (or any other science) has a personal meaning, because they've recorded their personal experiences with this subject throughout the year.

> Ms. Gallagher continues, "You will keep everything that you do in this class in your journal—notes, labs, homework, questions, projects, and reflections. Absolutely everything! I will make my handouts small enough so that you can tape them into your journal. So keep up."

We suggest to our students that they should keep their journals in chronological order. At the start of each class day, they should write the date and outline of the day's activities, which are listed on the board. Everything we do that day should be kept in their journal. Whenever we have a handout, we print it small enough so that students can tape it in their journals. Homework questions, lab sheets, project information, everything is taped chronologically into their journals. Not only does it keep the students organized, but it saves paper!

> "Remember, these are your journals. You're keeping a record of everything you do in here for the whole year."
>
> "Well, what if we run out of room? I write really big!" Monica says.
>
> "Good question! In the past, my students have put duct tape around the back cover of one journal and the front cover of another to, in essence, make one large journal! And two composition notebooks will be more than enough for the year."
>
> "Well, can we have one for each semester and just leave first semester's journal at home?" Erin asks.
>
> "Certainly," replies Ms. Gallagher. "However, students have shared with me in the past that it was helpful to have everything together.

Sometimes they needed to look something up from first semester, and it was beneficial to have both journals together."

"Do you grade these things?" Joe asks.

"Another good question," Ms. Gallagher responds. "No. This is your book. However, let me say three things. One, sometimes you are allowed to use your journal as a reference, so keeping a good record will be to your advantage. Two, sometimes I will ask you to recopy something from your journal onto separate paper so that I can collect it and grade that for accuracy. You're never to rip anything out of your journal. The better your record, the more accurate the information will be that you copy onto that separate sheet of paper. And three, in the past there has been a direct correlation between a very well kept journal and a high grade in my class. Just thought you might like to know!"

At this point, we show our students some previous journals from students, both good and bad. (Examples of student journals follow, Figures 4-1 through 4-9.) We point out what made a good journal—organization, detail, labeled pictures, thoroughness, etc. And then we talk about one other thing we want them to keep in their journals.

In terms of creating a scientific community, the journals play a key role. The only way our classes function as a community is if each member truly believes she or he has something worthwhile to offer the group. We have found the most effective way to accomplish this is to develop individual dialogue between each student and the teacher through the use of journals.

"But let's focus on the most important record that you will keep in your journal. This class will take on a personality that's quite unique from any other class. It will evolve and our community will grow. And the majority of the time we will function as a unit working together to explore and investigate. However, I am very much aware of the fact that this community is made up of distinct individuals. And I want to get to know you. Since we will be functioning as a group the majority of the time, it's difficult to get to know you as an individual during the class day. Therefore, I'd like to learn a bit about you by 'talking' with you through your journal.

"In order to accomplish this, every Friday, we will have a journal reflection question (see examples at end of this section). I will ask you to respond either to feedback I've given you, or to a question I've written on the board. I will collect your journals, read your response, and write back to you. That will be the start of our one-on-one conversation."

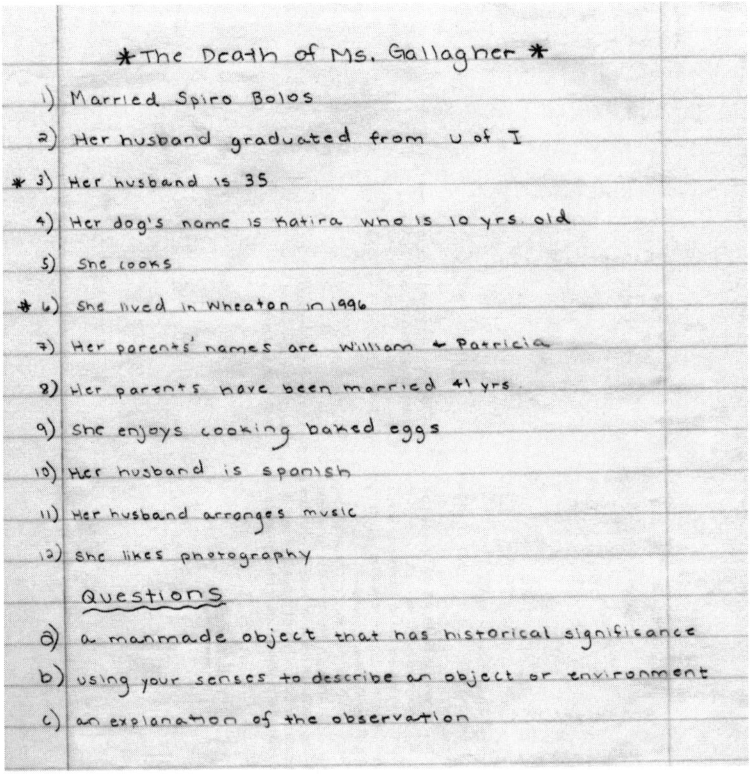

The Death of Ms. Gallagher

1) Married Spiro Bolos
2) Her husband graduated from U of I
* 3) Her husband is 35
4) Her dog's name is Katira who is 10 yrs old
5) She cooks
* 6) She lived in Wheaton in 1996
7) Her parents' names are William + Patricia
8) Her parents have been married 41 yrs.
9) She enjoys cooking baked eggs
10) Her husband is spanish
11) Her husband arranges music
12) She likes photography

Questions

a) a manmade object that has historical significance
b) using your senses to describe an object or environment
c) an explanation of the observation

Figure 4–1. *This is an example of a student journal entry during "The Death of Ms. Gallagher" activity.*

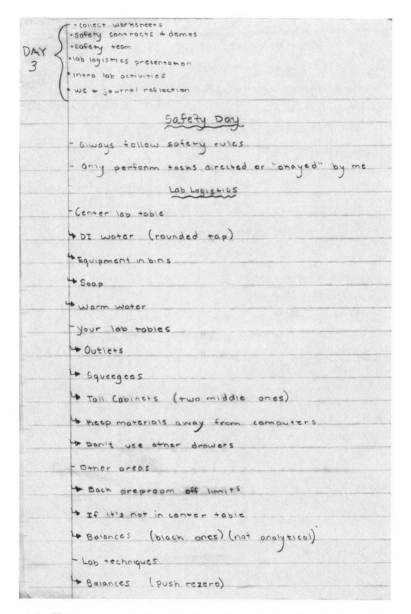

DAY 3
- collect worksheets
- safety contracts & demos
- safety team
- lab logistics presentation
- intro lab activities
- WS + journal reflection

Safety Day
- always follow safety rules
- Only perform tasks directed or "okayed" by me

Lab Logistics
- Center lab table
  ↳ DI water (rounded tap)
  ↳ Equipment in bins
  ↳ Soap
  ↳ Warm water
- Your lab tables
  ↳ Outlets
  ↳ Squeegees
  ↳ Tall Cabinets (two middle ones)
  ↳ keep materials away from computers
  ↳ Don't use other drawers
- Other areas
  ↳ Back preproom off limits
  ↳ If it's not in center table
  ↳ Balances (black ones) (not analytical)
- Lab techniques
  ↳ Balances (push rezero)

Figure 4–2. *This is an example of a student journal entry during the safety day training.*

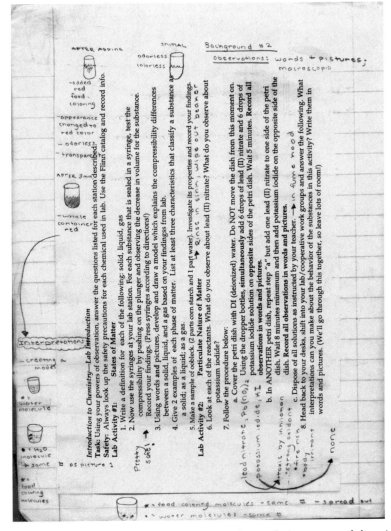

Figure 4–3a. *This is an example of a student journal entry during an expanded version of the Initial Lab Activity done after the safety day training. It is five pages and shows the start of getting students to model matter at the particulate level.*

Lab Activity #1:

1) solid: matter that has a definate shape + volume + is not compressible

liquid: a form of matter that flows, has a fixed volume, + takes the shape of its container + is not compress,

gas: a matter has no definite shape or volume; it adops the shape + volume of its container + is compressible

2) Gas compreses 8 mL

solid + liquid do not compress - stays at same volume

↳ when you pull out w/ liquid — it spreads to shape of container

3) gas

• = gas molecule
before compression

• = gas molecule
after compression

• = gas molecule - same # as before compression
The molecules are now closer together

liquid

o = liquid molecule
before compression

o = liquid molecule
after compression

- same # as before
- everything stayed the same

solid

O = solid molecule
before compression
- Have an order

O = solid molecule
after compression

- Everything stays the same

Figure 4–3b. *continued*

4) solid — ex. rock + pencil

liquid — ex. water + orange juice

gas — ex. oxygen + hydrogen

solid — definite shape, very slight expansion on heating, + almost incompressible

liquid — taking shape of its container, a fixed volume, + moderate expansion on heating

gases — an indefinite volume, great expansion on heating, + easy compressibility

5) oobleck *—sometimes a solid, sometimes a liquid: white, pasty liquid gooey, smells like cornstarch, looks like glue, sticky, clumpy, takes shape of container.

Lab Activity 2

6) lead (II) nitrate — looks like water, takes shape of container, clear, odorless

Figure 4–3c. *continued*

potassium iodide - looks like water, take shape of container, clear, transparant

a) before — clear, water

KI   Pb(no₃)₂

Immediately after adding 6 drops of both substances

· yellow iglittering arc
· definite lines between 2 substances
· KI is clear

after 5 min — · stayed the same as 3 min

Equation: $Pb(NO_3)_2 + KI \rightarrow KNO_3 + PbI$
(water)   Solid↑

what could happen:

before — · clear
immediately after — · still clear
after 3 minutes — · yellow solid sparkly line down middle

Figure 4–3d. *continued*

b)

• clear, water

• still clear, looks the same

before

after 8 min. + 6 drops of $Pb(NO_3)_2$

• glittery yellow blob

• lighter and less sparkly than part A

after adding 6 drops of KI

Conclusions:

★ • matter is made of discrete particles

• particles can move through water

• a different substance is formed from the original two

Figure 4–3e. *continued*

mole fraction = $\frac{moles\ water}{moles\ total}$

Colligative Properties
- Properties that depend on the number of particles (vapor pressure, rate of diffusion, freezing point, boiling point)
How will vapor pressure change for a liquid if it becomes a solution?

vapor pressure decreases when something's dissolved.

o = water
• = sugar

When you dissolve a substance into a liquid, the number of particles of the liquid at the surface decreases. This makes it more difficult for the particles to escape into the gas phase.

EX: → vapor pressure of water at 80°C (p.276) = 47.3 kPa
What is the vapor pressure of a solution with 45g of glucose dissolved in 108g of water at 80°C? $\left(\frac{6.000}{6.2500}\right)$ (47.34 kPa) = 45.4 kPa

Raoult's Law ⇒ Pressure of Solution = (mole fraction solvent)(v.P. of solvent)

$45.0g\ C_6H_{12}O_6 \times \frac{1\theta}{180g\ C_6H_{12}O_6\ C_6H_{12}O_6} = .2500$ $108.0g\ H_2O \times \frac{1\theta}{18.0g\ H_2O} = 6.000$

Figure 4–4. *This is an example of a student journal entry during a lecture on colligative properties. Notice the pictures drawn in order to continue to visualize matter at the particulate level.*

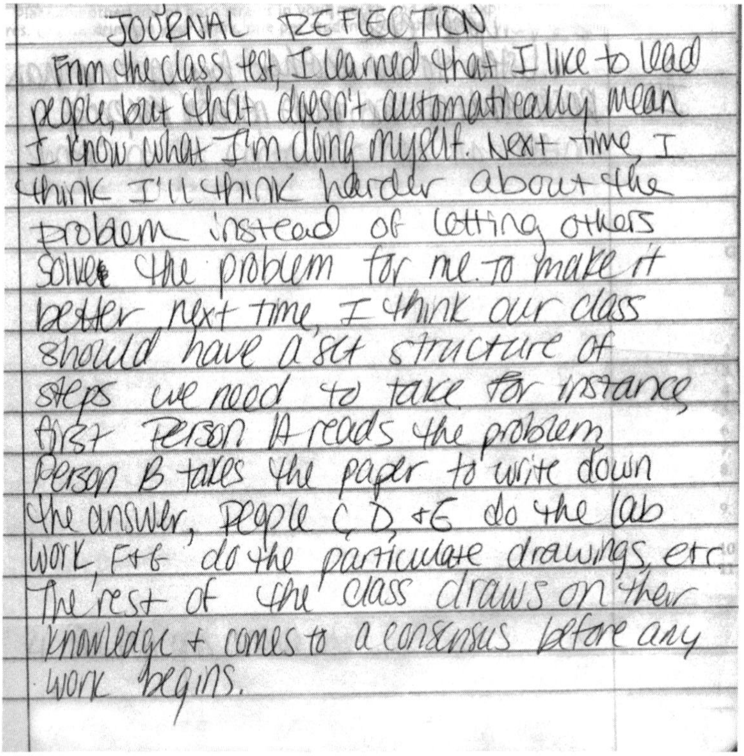

JOURNAL REFLECTION

From the class test, I learned that I like to lead
people, but that doesn't automatically mean
I know what I'm doing myself. Next time, I
think I'll think harder about the
problem instead of letting others
solve the problem for me. To make it
better next time, I think our class
should have a set structure of
steps we need to take for instance
first Person A reads the problem
Person B takes the paper to write down
the answer, People C, D, + E do the lab
work, F+G do the particulate drawings, etc.
The rest of the class draws on their
knowledge + comes to a consensus before any
work begins.

Figure 4–5. *This is an example of a student journal reflection response. The question asked was, "What did you learn from the first class test about yourself and how you work in a large group setting?"*

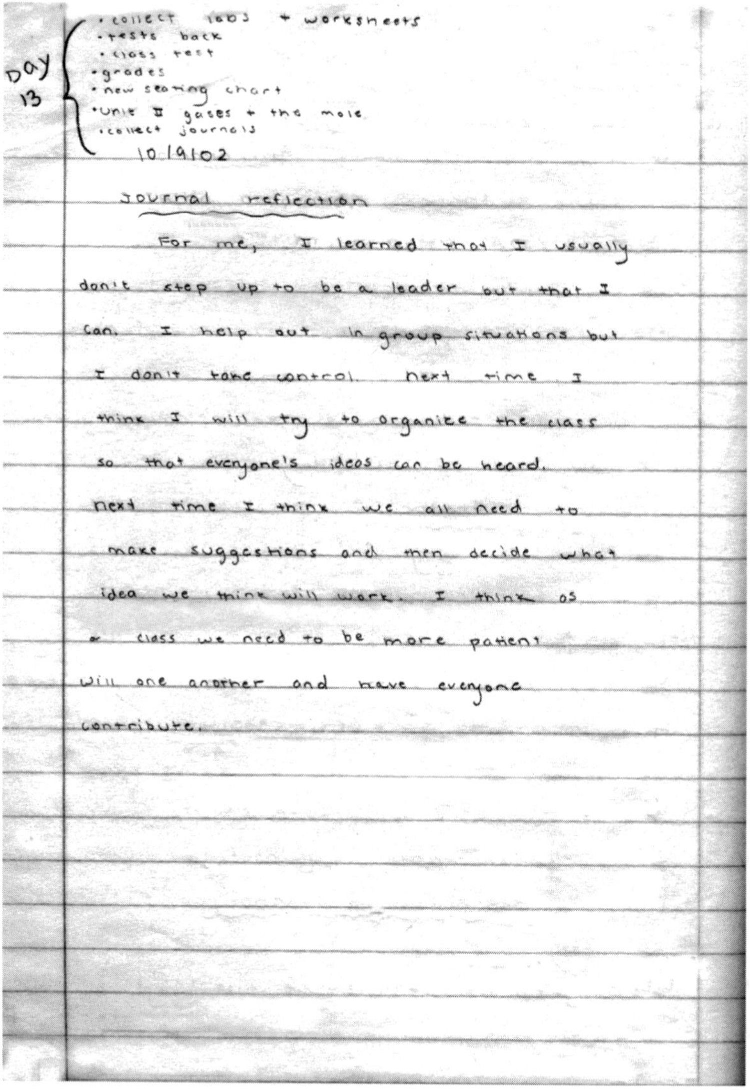

Day 13

- collect labs + worksheets
- tests back
- class test
- grades
- new seating chart
- Unit II gases + the mole
- collect journals

10/9/02

Journal reflection

For me, I learned that I usually don't step up to be a leader but that I can. I help out in group situations but I don't take control. next time I think I will try to organize the class so that everyone's ideas can be heard. next time I think we all need to make suggestions and then decide what idea we think will work. I think as a class we need to be more patient will one another and have everyone contribute.

Figure 4–6. *This is an example of a student journal reflection response. The question asked was, "What did you learn from the first class test about yourself and how you work in a large group setting?"*

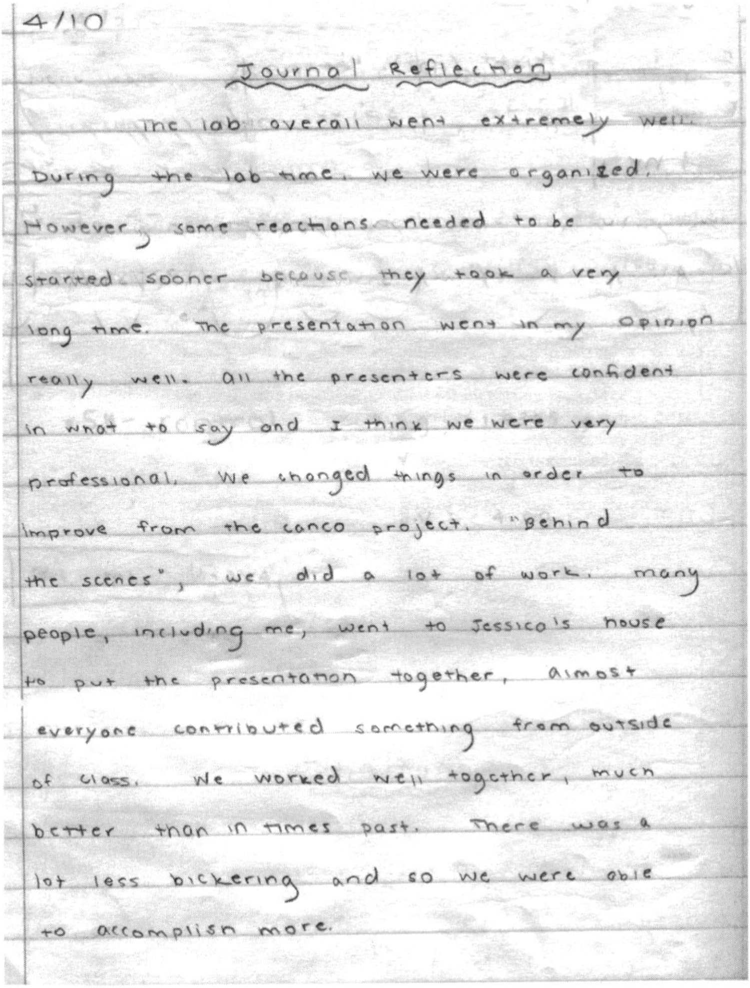

4/10

Journal Reflection

The lab overall went extremely well. During the lab time, we were organized. However, some reactions needed to be started sooner because they took a very long time. The presentation went in my opinion really well. All the presenters were confident in what to say and I think we were very professional. We changed things in order to improve from the conco project. "Behind the scenes", we did a lot of work. many people, including me, went to Jessica's house to put the presentation together. Almost everyone contributed something from outside of class. We worked well together, much better than in times past. There was a lot less bickering and so we were able to accomplish more.

Figure 4–7. *This is an example of a student journal reflection response. The question asked was, "How did the class lab go in terms of outside-of-class-time work?"*

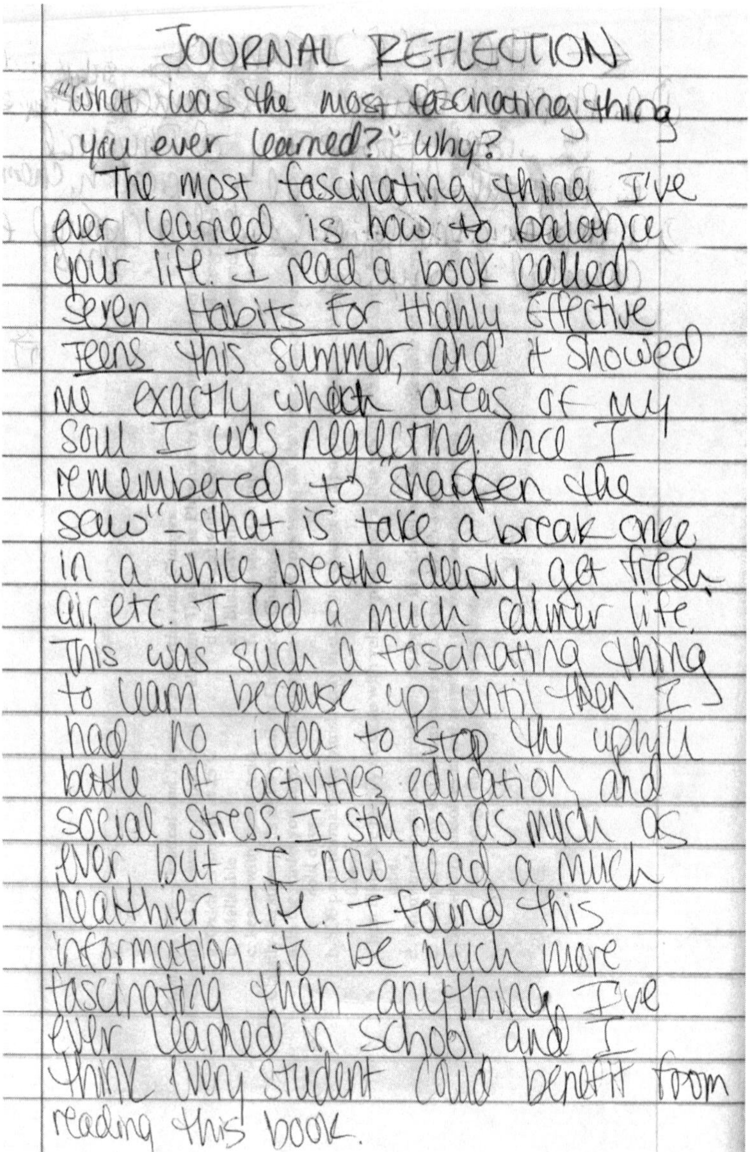

JOURNAL REFLECTION

"What was the most fascinating thing you ever learned?" why?

The most fascinating thing I've ever learned is how to balance your life. I read a book called Seven Habits for Highly Effective Teens this summer, and it showed me exactly which areas of my soul I was neglecting. Once I remembered to "sharpen the saw" - that is take a break once in a while breathe deeply, get fresh air, etc. I led a much calmer life. This was such a fascinating thing to learn because up until then I had no idea to stop the uphill battle of activities education and social stress. I still do as much as ever but I now lead a much healthier life. I found this information to be much more fascinating than anything I've ever learned in school and I think every student could benefit from reading this book.

Figure 4–8. *This is an example of a student journal reflection response. This was the first journal reflection question asked of students at the beginning of the year. The question asked was, "What was the most fascinating thing you ever learned?"*

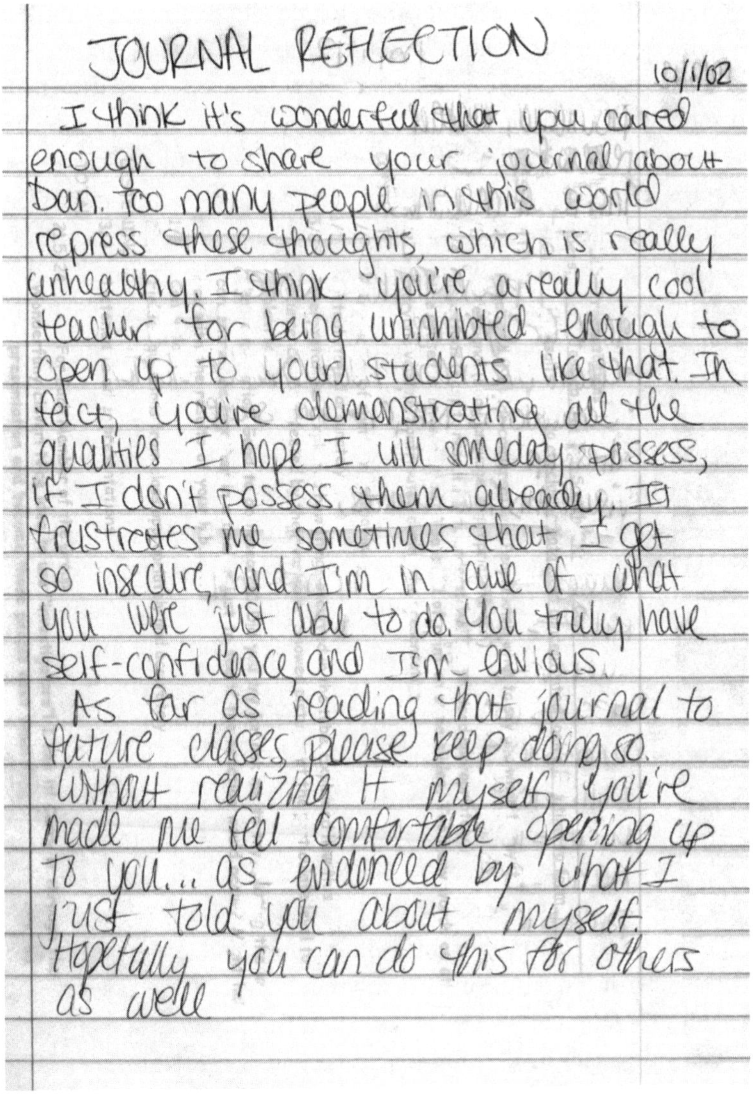

JOURNAL REFLECTION
                                              10/1/02

I think it's wonderful that you cared enough to share your journal about Dan. Too many people in this world repress these thoughts, which is really unhealthy. I think you're a really cool teacher for being uninhibited enough to open up to your students like that. In fact, you're demonstrating all the qualities I hope I will someday possess, if I don't possess them already. It frustrates me sometimes that I get so insecure, and I'm in awe of what you were just able to do. You truly have self-confidence and I'm envious.
   As far as reading that journal to future classes, please keep doing so. Without realizing it myself, you're made me feel comfortable opening up to you... as evidenced by what I just told you about myself. Hopefully you can do this for others as well

Figure 4–9. *This is an example of a student journal reflection response. It was in response to the journal that Ms. Gallagher had read to them. The question asked of her was, "What was the most difficult time in your life and how did you handle it?" Ms. Gallagher read a reflection that talked about the death of her friend. This is the student's response to that journal reading.*

So our students' journals not only include all the science—homework, notes, labs, questions, projects—but they also include these journal reflection responses. Again, these responses are our way of getting to know them individually. Students are much more comfortable writing things down as opposed to sharing them verbally in front of their peers, especially at the beginning of the year. We find that our student journal entries range from intriguing scientific phenomena to personal cries for help.

On the first Friday of the school year, we put up a journal reflection question (see "Sample Journal Reflection Questions," which follows), have the students respond in their journals, and then collect them. Over the weekend, we read their responses and write an individual note back to them. On Monday, we return their journals with their individual notes from us. The students appreciate the time we take to provide individual feedback and they quickly gain a respect for our position. They typically make a comment like "You wrote back to each of us! Wow! That must've taken you some time!"

You'll be amazed at how smoothly the classroom climate will develop once they receive their first feedback from the journal reflection. They're willing to try what you ask of them because you've shown them some individual respect. And even though some of the reflection questions are not directly related to science, the students are excited that there's a teacher who is concerned with them as people. We feel it's perhaps the most rewarding part of the job!

Sample Journal Reflection Questions

1. What is the most fascinating thing you ever learned (at home, in school, with a friend, on your own, at any age) that is somehow related to science? Why?
2. Respond to the feedback I just gave you.
3. What are three adjectives that describe who you are and what example can you give for each?
4. How does the word "density" relate to world population? What problems might exist with a high-density population?
5. Describe your weirdest experience. Make sure it's an appropriate story to share with the class.
6. If you discovered an element, what would you name it and why?

7. Respond to this statement: (Find something from the newspaper or media . . .)
8. What is your greatest fear? Why?
9. List three communities to which you belong. What have you done to be a contributing part of each community?
10. If all matter is made of particles, why is all matter so different?
11. What person or group of people are the most powerful in America? What evidence would you use to support your choice?
12. What is an item that you possess, one that you consider to be a luxury, that you would never give up? Why?
13. List the last three things that you said in your cooperative work group that were constructive. List the last three things that you said in your cooperative work group that were destructive/insulting. Comment on what types of reactions these statements would have evoked in you had you been on the receiving end of them.
14. If you were allowed only one method of communication, which one would you choose and why?
15. After you graduate from high school, what will be the one piece of advice you will give a friend, sibling, or loved one about high school?
16. Give me a story where you behaved like a scientist within the last week. This classroom doesn't count.
17. a. While working in your last cooperative work group, what did you learn about yourself? What's one thing you were really good at and one area that you found you needed to improve on?
    b. With this new cooperative work group, what are three areas that you could improve on while working with these members? How will you attempt to achieve these goals in the next three weeks?
18. What makes you happy?
19. If you could speak with one person in the world for 5 minutes, who would it be?

Safety

SEPT	Scientific Community	Safety

"As schools try to meet tough new science education standards set by the National Academy of Sciences in 1996, students are spending more time in the laboratories. Some are crowded. Some have teachers with no teacher safety training. Some are in 19th-century buildings ill-equipped for 21st-century science."[1] As stated in the Associated Press article, there are many reasons why the evidence shows an increase in the number of students getting hurt in science classrooms. "In Iowa, there were 674 accidents in the 1990, 1991, and 1992 school years, but more than 1,000 in the three following school years."[1]

With this dismal news, you may wonder how it is possible for your students to be in charge of the classroom, like we described in Chapter 2, while still maintaining a safe classroom. Safety issues can be difficult to monitor when you're in charge of a couple dozen students who have classroom freedom. Your first tendency might be to do fewer labs or to take control of the labs in terms of safety. We've learned that this is a mistake. It is our belief that by having the students in charge of their lab experiences, they will also be more likely to be in charge of the community's safety. Every member of the room needs to take responsibility for the safety of every other member of the room, obviously using the teacher's expertise as guidance. Most likely, many more injuries are occurring because there's no way teachers can possibly keep track of the actions of such a large group on their own.

At the high school level, this is typically not the students' first lab experience. However, it is their first experience in an environment with a record of so many accidents. They are around materials that deserve and demand respect, whether it be a biological, chemical, or physical science classroom. In addition, they are in a new room with a unique floor plan and unfamiliar safety equipment. They all need a thorough introduction. We spend a full day on lab safety, not only to further develop the importance of community, but to give our students the confidence and security that we care about keeping them safe.

We want our students in lab. Our students need to be in lab according to the *National Science Education Standards*. And it's our favorite part of teaching science! So there is a way to continue doing labs while keeping community safety the number one priority. The first step in getting the classroom set up safely is described in the following story.

"Who's the fastest runner in the room?" Ms. Gallagher asks.
    No response.

---

[1]Tammy Webber, Associated Press, 7/6/2002.

"Don't be shy. I want to know who can sprint the halls of this school faster than anybody else."

The students look around the room and start calling out names. It comes down to Brett and Brian.

Ms. Gallagher asks the two students, "So who is faster?" They can't decide. "OK, let's have a race down the hall." Brett wins.

Back in the classroom, Ms. Gallagher then designates Brett as the nurse runner. "Brett, should something happen to me during lab, sprint down to the nurse's office, tell her I need help, and get her back here quickly. I don't care if you have to carry her. But get medical help for me ASAP."

He smiles and says, "Sure thing. Will do." The rest of the class chuckles.

Then Ms. Gallagher goes through the rest of her security team assignments.

"Who is always in school?" A quick decision. "OK, Stephanie, if something happens to me during lab, you're in charge of calling 9-1-1. The closest phone is through that door in the lab prep room." Ms. Gallagher points. "But remember, it's not that easy! You must dial 9-9-1-1." The class chuckles. "So don't forget about the pressing two nines and two ones, OK?"

Stephanie smiles and says, "Got it!"

Ms. Gallagher continues, "Now, do you know the school address?"

Stephanie answers hesitantly, "Yeah. I think so."

Ms. Gallagher gasps in mock disbelief. "Wait! You have to be sure. I could really need some help!" The class laughs again. "Let me hear you say it." Stephanie rattles off the school address and room number, with help from other members of the room.

"Awesome! Now don't you forget that. So far I have my nurse runner and my 911 caller. Now for my third security team member . . . Who is good with names?" Another quick decision. "OK, Mike, if something happens to me, you go next door and get Ms. McDonaugh. Tell her I need help."

"Got it, Ms. Gallagher. That's easy."

"There's one more thing we need to cover. Let's make sure we all know how to use the fire extinguisher, safety blanket, eyewash, and shower." After Ms. Gallagher goes through the proper use of each piece of equipment, four individuals are designated in charge of that equipment. "If something happens to me, use the proper equipment and save me at all costs. And runners, do your jobs, no matter who's hurt. But remember, *use that equipment only if something has happened to me.* Otherwise, I'll use it. Nobody should ever be touching that equipment if I'm available to do so. Got it? OK, now let's practice." Ms. Gallagher yells, "Help! I'm on fire!"

The security team goes through a practice run. It takes Brett only twelve seconds to get to the nurse's office. He made sure to tell the nurse it was just a practice run. Stephanie pretends to call 9-1-1 by calling her house and rattling off the school address and room number to her mom, again giving the reassurance it was only for practice. Ms. McDonaugh appears in 5 seconds. And Ms. Gallagher was covered in a fire blanket before that by the appropriately assigned student. "Excellent! My two daughters will be pleased that you're all looking after me while I'm at work." The class applauds.

The preceding dialogue shows how we begin preparing the students to act safely in their lab explorations by assigning community safety responsibilities. We do the discussion in a fun and lighthearted manner, but the end conversation is always serious. Without the entire room involved with safety precautions, the security of the room falls apart. Somebody gets hurt. By allowing the students to actually practice safety responsibilities, they will know what to do in an emergency and they will understand that safety is of prime concern for everyone, not just the teacher.

Ms. Gallagher continues. "Remember that while you're working in lab, it is your responsibility to police each other at your designated lab table. If someone forgets goggles, a gentle reminder is needed. If someone is doing something that doesn't look like proper procedure, ask him or her a question. And most importantly, if your partner gets hurt, guide him or her to the proper piece of safety equipment while yelling my name, telling me what happened and where you're headed.

"For example, Annie and Mark, let's simulate the two of you working in lab." I whisper to Annie to pretend like she got something in her eye and to tell Mark what happened.

"Mark, I got some of this in my eye! It's burning!" she pretends to panic, pointing to one of the bottles on the table.

Ms. Gallagher explains, "Mark, you should then take her elbow and lead her to the eyewash while yelling for me. Make sure you know what she got in her eye, too, and let me know. So let's practice that." In four seconds all three of us are at the eyewash taking care of Annie's eye. "And what were the rest of you doing?" Ms. Gallagher asks the rest of the class.

"Getting out of your way!" Brett yells.

"Exactly. So don't wait for me to notice safety violations; it might be too late. Someone might be hurt. You always need to be following appropriate safety precautions. If I notice precautions not being taken, the community will forfeit its privilege of working in lab for that day. You didn't do what you needed to do to ensure the safety of all its members. But should someone get hurt, please do what we've practiced so we can prevent injuries from being serious."

The students in this classroom begin to see that safety is not just the responsibility of the teacher. They are all responsible. This is a very powerful message. We usually end up with at least one class having to sit out a lab due to too many reminders on the teacher's part to adhere to the safety precautions (see Handout 5—Science Laboratory Procedures and Contract). We typically allow three warnings during the first lab before asking them to sit down to review the importance. It's usually a goggle issue; for some reason, students take a while to get used to goggles in our chemistry classes. If the class has lost the privilege of being in lab, we have them watch us do the lab as a demo. They're obviously disappointed. But by removing them from the lab, they realize we're serious about safety and the community. And it never happens again. They police themselves quite well after that.

"Here's your eye." With gloved hands and goggled eyes, Mr. Smithenry holds up an egg.

"Here's sulfuric acid." He holds a beaker with concentrated sulfuric acid.

"Here's your eye in sulfuric acid!" He cracks the egg open and drops it into the acid. The raw egg begins to turn white.

"Any questions?" Mr. Smithenry looks at his students and smiles.

A few students comment, "Yuck! What's going on?"

"Is that egg being cooked?" Chris asks.

Brandon gasps. "Is that smoke coming from the beaker?"

"Those are some good questions. Yes, the egg is being cooked. And yes, I observed some smoke, too," Mr. Smithenry replies. His students are watching intently as he grabs another beaker with a clear liquid. "What common liquid could be in this beaker?"

"Water."

"Ethanol."

"Dead Sprite."

Mr. Smithenry nods. "Yes, those are all possible options. But notice that I am still wearing gloves and goggles, because watch what this liquid does to this paper towel." He takes a stirring rod, dips it into the liquid, and rubs it onto the paper towel. The towel begins to turn black immediately and falls apart where the liquid was in contact. "This beaker contains sulfuric acid, the same liquid that just cooked the egg. What do these two demos tell you about the dangers of concentrated sulfuric acid?"

"It would probably hurt if you got it in your eye," says Rachel.

"It wouldn't be good to get it on your skin," adds Jason.

"It will cook things!" Mark comments.

"And that's the reason for the goggles and gloves. 'Have a healthy respect for chemicals' is my motto and one that you will share as you begin to investigate in the lab. Even though you may think something is just water, it could be a potentially very dangerous chemical. Safety gear can protect you from dangers in the lab, especially when the things surrounding you are seemingly safe."

Prior to this lesson, all of our students have signed a safety contract, cosigned by parents (see Handout 5—Science Laboratory Procedures and Contract). Now they've seen demos to illustrate exactly what the contract was referring to. We have our safety team in place. So to conclude this lesson, we get our students into an introductory lab experience. It is now time to test our classes to see if they are ready to police themselves as a community in a lab experience.

Handout 5—Science Laboratory Procedures and Contract

Ms. Gallagher—Glenbrook North High School

The science laboratory is a place of adventure and discovery. Some of the most important events in history have happened in laboratories. However, the laboratory can be potentially dangerous if proper safety rules are not followed at all times. In order to prepare yourself for a safe year in the laboratory, read over the following safety rules. Then read them again. Make sure you understand each rule. Sign and date the contract in the space provided and turn this sheet into me at the end of the hour today.

Before every lab, read directions carefully. Make sure you understand the overall picture before beginning. Ignorance is dangerous!

1. Make sure equipment is clean before every experiment.
2. Gather all equipment before beginning experiments and bring it to your station.
3. Always wear safety goggles. Also, contact lens wearers need to notify me before every lab. Irritation can be caused by some fumes.
4. Tie back long hair and loose clothing to keep them away from chemicals and flames. No hats allowed in lab! No sitting in lab!
5. Never eat or drink in lab. Not even gum! Especially not gum!
6. Never touch, taste, or smell any chemical unless instructed to do so. To note an odor, gently wave your hand over the opening of the container to direct the fumes toward your nose and smell carefully.
7. Never perform unauthorized activities; listen to the teacher.
8. If spills occur, ask your teacher about proper cleanup. Don't assume something on the lab table is water, even if it looks that way. Tell me!
9. Hot glassware or burners will not appear hot. Check before touching.
10. Report all accidents/injuries to your teacher immediately! Even if you don't think it's bad enough to report, report it!
11. Dispose of chemicals as instructed by your teacher.
12. If you have trouble lighting a Bunsen burner, turn off gas immediately. Ask for my help.
13. Never return chemicals to the stock bottle.
14. Always point a test tube or container that is being heated away from you and others.
15. If a container had a lid or stopper on it before you used it, close the container securely when you are finished, even if someone is waiting to use the same bottle behind you.
16. When diluting concentrated acids, always pour acid into water. Never water into acid.
17. Clean up your lab station and all equipment after the experiment, return all equipment to the proper place, and turn off all burners and hot plates.

18. Wash your hands after each experiment!
19. Note the location of the fire extinguisher, fire blanket, eyewash station, and shower.
20. If something happens to the teacher, the appointed students should do their jobs (teacher next door, nurse, call 911, safety equipment experts).

Student Name (Print) _____ Class_____

Student Signature_____ Date_____

"Here's today's lab activity." Ms. Gallagher hands out a lab description (see Handout 6—Chemical Changes Lab). "Before actually going back to do the lab, I need someone to volunteer to look up the safety precautions for the chemicals that we'll be using back there. Today's chemicals are 0.5 M lead (II) nitrate and 0.5 M potassium iodide."

Erica jumps up, grabs the *Flinn* catalog out of Ms. Gallagher's hand, and finds the hazards listed under each chemical. "I found them, Ms. Gallagher. What do I do with them?"

"Write them on the board for all of us to record in our journals." Erica writes on the board that there are no hazards for potassium iodide and that lead nitrate is a fire risk and it is toxic by inhalation and ingestion.

Ms. Gallagher then places two bottles of solid lead nitrate and solid potassium iodide on the front lab table next to the solutions of each. "This is how I purchased them," she says, pointing to the bottles filled with solids, "but this is what they look like for your use today. How did I get from solid form to 'liquid' form?"

Jennifer hesitantly answers, "You added water?"

"Exactly. So that slightly changes our safety precautions because the ones that are written on the board are for the solid form. Is it as easy to ingest or inhale this solution as it would be in the solid form? No, of course not; a powder might fly in the air when you open the bottle and in the solution the solid has been diluted. Is it as flammable in solution? No, of course not. But what happens if we spill this on the lab table and the water evaporates? You are left with the solid lead nitrate and its hazards. So if you spill this, wipe it up with a paper towel. You cannot leave it on the lab surface. By the way, where should we dispose of our products?" Ms. Gallagher asks.

"Well, since you asked the question, I'm betting that the answer is not 'down the sink,'" Kevin offers. The class chuckles.

"Good answer," Ms. Gallagher says with a smile. She writes the chemical reaction for this lab on the board and points out lead iodide as one of the products. "This needs to go into the waste container in the fume hood. We will have to pay to get rid of it at the end of the year."

As described, students got a chance to research the hazards associated with the chemicals in this lab. (We have them do this before each lab activity throughout the year. We also discuss what to do in case there is an accident with a particular chemical.) You can choose any initial activity for your class. We suggest you pick one that uses relatively safe materials so that you can see if your students have developed a mature respect for the room and each other. We use Handout 6—Chemical Changes Lab for our chemistry classes.

During this initial activity, it is interesting to take pictures and/or video footage of the students' first lab experience with you. We then look at these the next day and have the students pick out all the safety hazards. We mention that violations like those in the pictures might prevent them from being in lab in the future. They need to police each other to maintain a safe community.

Handout 6—Chemical Changes Lab

Objectives

1. To identify when a chemical reaction takes place based on observations.
2. To record observations and interpretations using words and pictures.
3. To become familiar with how chemicals react.

   What are the characteristics of a chemical change?
   How can drawing pictures help us learn what takes place during a chemical reaction?

Techniques

1. To practice beginner safety procedures.
2. To properly dispose of all chemicals. (Take a mental picture of the lab when you walk in. The lab should be left the same way.)

Safety background

You should always look up and record the hazard alerts and disposal methods associated with the chemicals we're using in an activity or lab. The best place to find this information is in the *Flinn Scientific Catalog* located on the front lab table. If there is an unknown in the lab, you should consult me for this information! Lead (II) nitrate $[Pb(NO_3)_2]$ and potassium iodide [KI] are the chemicals used in today's activity.

Task

- What observations can you make following the procedures listed below? Record all observations throughout the activity, in words and pictures.

Procedure

1. Cover the bottom of the petri dish with DI water. From this moment on do not move or shake the dish. Using the dropper bottles, simultaneously add 6 drops of lead (II) nitrate solution and 6 drops of potassium iodide solution on opposite sides of the petri dish. Wait for at least 5 minutes before proceeding to step 2.
2. In another petri dish, repeat step 1 but instead of adding both chemicals at the same time, add the potassium iodide solution five minutes after you add the lead (II) nitrate solution.
3. Dispose of all solutions as instructed by your teacher.

Questions

Answer the following in your journal.

1. How were the results for each petri dish different? similar?
2. What interpretations can you make about the behavior of the substances in this activity? Record in words and pictures. Use the demo done earlier in class as a guide.

Chemical changes lab

(teacher information)

MAIN GOAL

Getting students to think of matter as particles.

LAB SETUP

Use 0.5 M solutions for both KI and $Pb(NO_3)_2$. Have a waste container available for the PbI_2 precipitate. Consult a *Flinn* catalog for disposal.

PRELAB DISCUSSION

1. Emphasize to the students the importance of trying to visualize what is happening in the lab at the particulate level. Tell them to interpret their observations using dots in their sketches to represent the particles.
2. Tell the students to perform the lab, document their findings, and then walk around and look at each lab group's results.

POSTLAB DISCUSSION

The questions outlined on the student sheet should be done as homework so as to give the students time to reflect on what they think happened in lab. The discussion on the next day can follow the outline below.

1. Have each lab group put their sketches of the interpretations from procedures #1 and #2 on the board.
2. Have one member of each group explain his or her interpretation of procedures #1 and #2 to the class.
3. Ask the class for a list of key ideas of all the interpretations upon which they can agree.
4. It is not necessary to get involved with the discussion of the separation of the ionic compounds into ions in solution. This concept is beyond the scope of the objectives for this lab.
5. Hopefully at the end of this discussion, students will be talking about these ideas:

   a. Matter is made of discrete particles.
   b. Particles can move through water.
   c. A different substance is formed from the original two.

Cooperation

SEPT	*Scientific Community*	*Cooperation*

The last step in setting up the scientific community in the classroom is to focus on cooperation. The students must learn to trust one another and work constructively together in order to eventually accept the responsibility of running the classroom. We begin to ease up on the reins by giving some freedom to the community in order to plan, implement, and analyze an experiment.

Our focus on cooperation begins with the lab described in Handout 7—Ammonia and Hydrochloric Acid Lab. Remember, in the Chemical Changes Lab, all students were gathering and recording the same information. The Ammonia and Hydrochloric Acid activity requires a group of students to collect unique information and then share it with the rest of the community. Based on the shared information, the class will be given a task that requires a cooperative group effort to succeed.

We begin the activity by doing a simple demonstration. The teacher places a blue Q-tips® swab in NH_3 and a pink Q-tips in HCl. She places both Q-tips in opposite ends of a glass tube at the same time. Then the students observe a white precipitate form near the pink Q-tips. This is where the experiment begins for the students.

We choose this lab because it easily allows one lab group the opportunity to test a unique variable from any of the other lab groups. It lends itself well to the idea of a true experiment, where not even the teacher will know the exact outcome of the variables being tested. It is an inquiry-based lab and provides a good foundation for questions initiated by the students as to what really makes up matter. It is a perfect transition into our next unit, which focuses on the particulate nature of matter—specifically those in the gas phase, as is true in this lab. But most importantly, it requires the students to work together to "figure out" what really affects the formation of the white ring. (The entire lab handout follows, with a follow-up story to illustrate how it's played out in the classroom.)

Handout 7—Ammonia and Hydrochloric Acid Lab

Objectives

1. To become familiar with mapping out variables.
2. To become accustomed to working in a group environment.
3. To effectively communicate group results to an audience.
4. To apply knowledge gained from lab to a practical exam.
5. To write a quality, formal lab report.

Techniques

To learn to handle potentially dangerous chemicals in the appropriate manner . . . in the fume hood.

Safety background

The substances in this lab are concentrated hydrochloric acid [HCl] and concentrated ammonium hydroxide [NH_3].

Task

After the initial activity, what variables do you think affected the observed results?

Initial activity—Procedure

Record all observations in your journal throughout the lab! Details, details, details.

1. Gather one glass tube, one pink cotton swab, one blue cotton swab, and two pairs of gloves. Prepare equipment as demonstrated.
2. Take a pink cotton swab and place five drops of HCl on it (as demonstrated by your teacher).
3. Take a blue cotton swab and place five drops of NH_3 on it (as demonstrated by your teacher).
4. At the same time, place each cotton swab in opposite ends of the glass tube. Bring back to your lab table.

5. Dispose of chemicals and cotton swabs as instructed by your teacher! Rinse glass tube with water and bring to fume hood.

Questions

Respond to the following in your journals.

1. Write down your initial interpretations (pictures and words) in order to answer the following questions:

   a. Where did the solid come from?
   b. How did it get there?
   c. Why did the solid form the way it formed in each step?

Ammonia and Hydrochloric Acid Lab—Follow-Up

Follow-up task

Each group will test one of the variables discussed today. Write up a plan in your journal for tomorrow's lab. Your plan should include, but not be limited to, how you will test the connection between your variable and the observed results from today's activity. It must be done by each person and must be preapproved before you can enter the lab.

Presentations

Each lab group will then present its findings to the rest of the class using at least one visual aid. Every member of the group must be part of the presentation.

Class challenge

Based on the information the class gathered, the class must get the precipitate to form in the middle of a designated tube.

Homework

A lab report is due. It should include information from your lab tests (the variable that your group tested, NOT the initial activity or the class challenge).

After the demo, Ms. Gallagher asks, "What are some things that may have affected the way the precipitate formed?" She invites all responses and records them on the board.

"The temperature of the room."

"The size of the tube."

Ms. Gallagher says, "Define size."

One student responds, "How long it is."

Another one adds, "How fat it is."

"Great. Any others?"

"The amount of liquid on the Q-tips."

"What if you didn't put them in at the same time?"

After a number of variables are listed on the board, Ms. Gallagher asks the students to decide which variable they think should be and/or could be tested safely and effectively in the lab. The class decides on six variables and each group volunteers to test one. (These are the same groups from the last lab.)

"So are we ready to go? Can we start?" asks Ms. Gallagher.

The majority of the class responds, "Yep."

Ms. Gallagher says, "Take a minute to picture yourself in lab and think about anything else we need to discuss. Focus on the word *variable* while you are thinking."

Natalie says, "Don't we need to set up a control?"

With direction, the students decide what the class control should be. Every group will use the same control, but each lab group will test one variable. The class remembers that they must look up safety hazards. The class records them, asks about disposal procedures, and appears ready to go. Ms. Gallagher repeats the variable that each group should test and then says, "Get busy."

The students eagerly break up into their lab groups to test their variables because they decided on them. They own their variable. Certainly it's possible that they will realize some of their choices were poor ones. But that is all part of learning how to plan an effective experiment. After testing begins, they are to document their observations and will be responsible, as a group, to present their findings to the rest of the class using at least one visual aid. It is expected that each member of the community will understand the results presented for every variable from each group. We encourage the class to ask questions of the presenters until they are comfortable with the information.

"Now that you've heard the conclusions from each group, this is your class challenge. Using this particular glass tube, get the precipitate to form exactly in the center. You have exactly twenty minutes to accomplish this task. Before you go into the lab, as a class, you may ask me two questions, and I reserve the right not to answer them. So think carefully."

Susie asks, "So we can ask you two questions?"

"Yes. That was number one. What's your second question?" Ms. Gallagher laughs.

A few groans are heard. A student says out loud, "Is that really one of our questions?"

Ms. Gallagher asks, "Are you speaking to me?"

The whole class yells, "No! She wasn't asking you. That was definitely not a question!"

Ms. Gallagher smiles and says, "OK, you now have only nineteen minutes left. Get busy!"

The class gets focused and busy. Nineteen minutes pass. The students turn in their tube. The bell rings. Class is over.

During the class challenge, definitions of "focused and busy" vary wildly from class to class. In one class, one student may take charge while the rest of the class blindly follows. In another, six students might try to dominate all decisions while others are passive. Still in a third, nobody takes charge and the class hesitantly throws something together at the end. And sometimes, a class will amaze you with its natural organization and drive.

"Let's talk about yesterday's class challenge. First, who has questions on the chemistry content because I will freely answer any of those." Ms. Gallagher explains how some of the variables may have affected the precipitate formation. Her more important focus is on how they cooperated with one another without the teacher in charge.

"OK, let's not focus on chemistry. Let's focus on how well you worked together as a class. What worked well? What would you do differently? Take three minutes and write five things down in your journal and then we will talk."

Discussions will range from being extremely negative to incredibly positive, depending on what happened in class. We like to keep the discussion as positive as we can; remember, this was their first try at working together with minimal direction under time constraints. Keep the class focused on analyzing how they worked together and on coming up with concrete methods for improving for their next challenge. One example of guiding the class to a concrete solution is given below.

> Ms. Gallagher shares, "In my experience, it's always good to have two class managers. One isn't enough; it's too much pressure. And three or more is too confusing. It's a suggestion to make sure that one of your managers feels very comfortable in front of his peers and a second manager feels comfortable thinking chemistry on his feet. Can I have six nominations on the board?"

We could get caught up in giving the class more than one hundred ways to improve for the next challenge. However, the process of letting go takes months. So we have them practice only a few pieces of the puzzle each time they do a class activity, giving them a bit more freedom each time. These are the four points we have the students focus on after this initial opportunity of performing a class challenge on their own. All are important, but the fourth one seems to help students the most.

1. You must have class managers when you are in charge of the classroom.
2. Everyone must take an active role in accomplishing a class task.
3. Nobody gets left behind. It's more important to stay together than to finish the job.
4. You have to be comfortable with being confused. Remember, you are all in the same boat. I wouldn't give you a challenge that I didn't think you could successfully accomplish together. It's supposed to be difficult, but it will always be doable if you cooperate!

We give the students all three areas of feedback, as mentioned in Chapter 3—safety, accuracy, and community. The first two are obviously important in the science classroom. They actually don't take much time to go through, since the students have focused on them so much already in this activity. The community part, especially this early in the school year, takes a bit of time. And we emphasize the four preceding points because our experience—trial and error—shows these to be the most helpful at this point in the year.

In Chapter 2 we described what you want your classroom to look like by the end of the year. In Chapter 4, we've given you the way to start the year off on the right path toward that end. You need to continue to use these five ideas we've presented—class climate, trust, journals, safety, and cooperation—throughout the year, giving the students a bit more freedom each time you put them in charge. These five ideas become the foundation to our scientific community. We refer back to this first week of school all year long, in order to remind our students about the importance of working together. These ideas have come from experience both in academia and in industry. With them firmly in place we can then prepare our students to accomplish similar and even more challenging tasks, without our direct guidance. This is our goal.

In Chapter 5 we share with you concrete examples of activities that we use throughout the year. These lead the class on the path to becoming a self-sufficient scientific community.

SEPT	*Scientific Community*
OCT	*Part. Nature of Matter & Gas Laws*
NOV	*Atomic Structure & Per. Trends*
DEC	*Reactions & Stoich.*
JAN	*Stoich.*
FEB	*Equilibrium & Thermo-chemistry*
MAR	*Acids & Bases*
APR	*Organic*
MAY	*Soap*
JUNE	*Finals*

Class Assessments and Projects Throughout the Year

5

So What Happens Throughout the Year?

Up to now, we've discussed the end of the year project (Chapter 2) and the beginning of the year (Chapter 4). In this section we want to fill in the gap by giving the reader six examples of class assessments and projects that are done over the course of the year. The assessments are one day in length, while the projects are longer, two to three days. These assessments and projects are designed to gradually give the students more responsibility, freedom, and practice in accomplishing a given class task as a community. As mentioned earlier, these types of community activities are not stand-alone, but supplemented by traditional teaching methods.

Our first example is taken from the gas unit covered in October. The first activity is a three-day project based on the familiar "can-crushing" demo, where a soda can is heated with water and is crushed by quickly inverting it into a cold water bath. This is the first project where the students are in charge for an extended period. For the three days of class, there is no prompting from the real teacher (but with help from a "consultant," Ms. Nac, role-played by the teacher). It is up to the students to organize and plan for themselves how to accomplish a given task. The challenge is huge, but one that shows them we are serious about trusting them to be in charge. To give the reader an idea of what happens in our classrooms during this project, we provide two example teacher journal entries recorded while doing this project. One illustrates what happened in a regular-level chemistry class, and the other an honors chemistry class.

CanCo Project

OCT	Part. Nature of Matter & Gas Laws	CanCo Project

"Good morning. My name is Dr. Fox (character role-played by the teacher). I am CanCo's company president. I am here today looking to hire a scientific community that can prove that it is able to effectively and efficiently solve CanCo's technical research problems. You can prove your community's worth by solving the problem outlined in this handout (see Handout 8—CanCo Project—at the end of this section) and giving a twenty-minute presentation to me on the assigned deadline. I will supply one of my company's chemists, Ms. Nac, to act as a consultant while you perform your experiments. She will help only when asked a question. She may not be able to answer all questions, but she will try."

At this point, "Dr. Fox" leaves the room and puts on a new name tag, "Ms. Nac." The teacher reenters the room with a computer, sits in the back of the room, and listens to the students planning their next moves. We type what we hear and see (and what we want to tell them later). And if the students ask "Ms. Nac" a question, the teacher stays in character as the company chemist and answers content and technique questions only. Ms. Gallagher, the real teacher, does not exist for the next two and a half days. The following example describes a three-day journal of Joan's observations. A second journal example from a different class follows.

Remember that two class managers were chosen in September. They know that when a class task is given, that they need to stand up and try their best to manage the room without the aid of the teacher. The teacher does not divulge any specific information to these class managers prior to the actual activity. It is understood and well practiced at this point that the class managers are there to help the journey go more smoothly by organizing the class as best they can. Katie and Brett were class managers at the time this activity took place in October.

Example Teacher Journal 1

Day 1

I am impressed that Katie and Brett immediately had the class focused on the first question, "What variables affect the amount of the can crush?" You listed as many as you could. You wrote them down in your journals. You all did a nice job assigning tasks and got busy in lab. You worked through the hour and cleaned up. Nice job. But I'm not sure that the data you collected was actually going to help you solve the problem . . . We'll see . . .

Day 2

Brett immediately asked if any group had a need to do further testing. Nobody did, apparently. (I was surprised that all groups said they were done. Suggestions: Remember that you have to have enough data to "prove your case." Also, please make sure you always do a few "extreme" trials.)

So Brett said, "OK, let's write your best results on the board." This took a bit of effort on his part to get everyone to figure out the best crush in terms of percentage. Suggestion: For all class members, if you had no further testing, you should've come prepared to class with that information. Just because I didn't give any homework does *not* mean that there's no homework to be done. And to the managers, anticipate this type of thing. If there's no outline on the board, plan for the next class and put one there when you walk into class. You should come to class prepared to write designated jobs on the board. So there's your homework . . .

One variable needed further testing. So you boiled some water and tested the water bath temperature really high. This proved to be a worse outcome than the 43°C water. So you went back to using that. You asked Ms. Nac if that was a good decision. She asked if you had ever tried the other extreme. You hadn't, so you did. Good for you. Ms. Nac gave you a suggestion and you followed through.

It was decided that the "best variables" would be tested in order to determine whether they would get consistent results. They used ice water and tried both 10 and 30 mL. They may have tried more, but I got distracted by the number of people doing absolutely nothing! The five people in back doing the lab are focused. Suggestion: Again, if you're not designated a job, figure something out that you can do, make the suggestion to your manager, and see if she or he approves. Then get busy. Trust me, there's lots to do. Managers, give chores! Again, had you planned out the day, then the rest of the class would have work to do. Both ends let each other down. But not for very long!

Many teachers might assume that simply because students got off task or unfocused that this was a waste of time. As we addressed earlier, at least we know which students are not focused by the very nature of this kinesthetic, hands-on activity. As opposed to demo-ing or lecturing, we can actually see and hear who's doing what.

There are ways to direct your class to really attack a challenge, even during moments of confusion. Since this is the beginning of the year, it is still new to them. If things are really bad, interjecting hints or asking questions while walking around the room as Ms. Nac has worked for us. Another idea is to give them an open-journal pop quiz the next day. This will really drive home the importance of working together and sharing information. But spending a significant amount of time anticipating and/or focusing on the moments when things get offtrack does very little good. The preceding journal entry reflects a fleeting moment of disappointment by the teacher. The students heard about it during feedback, and things changed quickly in the next class task.

Day 2 Continued

The class continued to test things together. A few interesting thoughts were posed in reference to your data:

Someone said at one point, "30 mL is too inconsistent. Let's use 10 mL." That's a wonderful observation. Does anyone know why? Is anyone thinking through what's happening here? Why do you think I had you draw pictures of eggs in bottles and two-liter bottles the day before this lab? Can you model this behavior?"

During this second day, I saw a few moments of community breakdown. This was due to laziness. There were so many things that these people could have done to improve things for the good of the community. Don't limit yourselves to do just what's told. Think. Be creative. When you're given this kind of freedom, fly with it . . .

There are moments, many moments throughout the year, where we feel compelled to jump in and provide guidance. Through experience, we've found that doing this completely undermines the goal of getting the students to take charge for themselves. Instead, it makes them depend on us for things that we know they are capable of doing when given the chance. We find it incredibly draining to keep quiet, but we let our students fall. We let them make mistakes. Students are very frustrated with confusion. We give them the opportunity to realize that it's important to be comfortable with confusion, as long as they learn to formulate questions, know where to go to answer these questions, and work together toward solving the tasks at hand. In addition we will help them develop these skills as the year progresses by providing feedback following every activity.

Day 3

Day 3 was a bit confusing at the beginning. But soon there were some good dialogues taking place and the managers were trying to get people focused. But 30 minutes into class, Cassandra was up at the board writing, Brett is nowhere to be seen, and the class is not focused. Then Brett appeared and things turned around when a practice run of the presentation was started. This was a great idea. It was wonderful for the whole class to hear what each lab group representative had to say and then for the class to give feedback in order to improve for the real thing. Nice work. You finished on a strong note . . .

This example of the teacher's observations shows that the students are working together on tasks, but still need help with organization and management. They are slowly becoming more comfortable taking ownership of the classroom.

The following is another example of a three-day journal entry, written while observing the same project done by another class. You'll notice organizational confusion in both, but each class handles it in a different manner. Therefore, different thoughts enter our minds as we observe. Each class eventually succeeds in all three areas: climate, content, and safety. (Jeff and Julia are the class managers.)

Example Teacher Journal 2

Day 1

Jeff and Julia got up to help organize the class. Good for you. Planning is the key. Let's see what you come up with.

Jeff breaks up the class into six groups. The groups head to the back of the room. Jeff tells them to bring cans to their respective lab tables to begin testing how to best crush them. The whole class gets up and heads to their lab stations to begin working.

Julia reminds the class that each group should test the control at the beginning. Nice! Of course they should. But do you even have variables assigned yet? Have you decided on a control as a class yet? I certainly didn't hear it! So what is everyone doing back in lab? What are you testing and recording?

After a few minutes, the class heads back to their desks. Good. You realized that you had absolutely *no* organization. Nobody knew what to do! With this many questions flying around the room and this level of obvious confusion, you need to plan better.

This is one of those moments where we want to jump in and give direction. But we hold back, for the reasons already mentioned. We need to give them the time to feel confused, get comfortable with their confusion, and then learn how to formulate the question that will move them forward.

Your discussion at your desks gets underway. Jonie wants to know what the control is. Wonderful! Elliot wants a standard procedure . . . Excellent! And many in the room are asking what each group should test as a variable. Yes!

Jeff then asks the class—or himself; I'm not sure—"What would cause the pressure on the inside to decrease?" That's it, Jeff! Can you answer that? If you can, you've got the key! And you'll have figured out what variables to assign.

Elliot almost hits it by saying, "Get it hotter, then cool it down fast." Intuitively, you're understanding this. But can you take it that one step that will make the difference? You're so close, I want to jump in! But I won't. I want you to figure it out and then share it with the class. Let's see what happens. Keeping thinking!

At this point, the class is talking a mile a minute. Andrew reminds the class to raise hands when they want to talk, not to interrupt each other.

> Then Jeff wrote the ideal gas law on the board. Wow! You're think-
> ing! Has the rest of the class read this information yet? It's wonderful
> that you have and that you're explaining it to the class!

And there are moments where our students amaze us. Here Jeff
made a connection between the lab activity and the textbook content
without me saying a single word. He intuitively made the connection; his challenge is to explain it to his peers, which he does amaz-
ingly well.

> The class concludes its discussion on a control and which variables each
> group will test. You also decided on what information each group
> should record. Elliot, did you get your standard procedure? I didn't see
> it! I saw remnants of one, but nothing clear-cut. Anyway, you all went
> back to lab to begin your respective tests.
>
> I hear someone mentioning safety. Good. Anna saved Kierstyn by
> reminding her to put goggles on before entering lab! Way to go.
>
> A cluster of people are up front. Lots of questions about the
> "depth" variable. I have a question or two about it, too. And again, peo-
> ple raising issues with what exactly needs to be recorded. All testing
> ceases again as the class stands in lab debating the same issues you had
> apparently cleared up earlier. What's going on?
>
> Rajal wants to get a definition of each variable cleared up. In par-
> ticular, she wants "depth" explained. Good. You're formulating ques-
> tions at the point of confusion. What a wonderful skill to possess!
>
> The class is getting frustrated with Jeff. In his defense, it's really
> tough to interpret all the info flying at him. Some of the questions are
> tough to figure out, let alone answer to an entire class at once. But I do
> agree that it's important to stop standing around debating. You need to
> get some tests done. You're doing much better than you think, though.
> I can tell! I'm wondering where you will go from here? What will you
> do with your frustration? Who will actually take the lead and give
> direction?

In many instances it appears that our classes are spiraling out of
control and they look to the back of the room for our guidance. But
the students soon realize that we're not going to help them out of their
mess (as long as their safety is not compromised, of course).
Eventually, somebody figures out that the class needs to sit, think, and
get organized, and they do it. And sometimes, with these beginning-

of-the-year projects, this realization happens after we read these journals to them, along with supplementary feedback. Either way, our students become better prepared for their next independent class/community/company project.

Day 1 Continued

With only 5 minutes left in class, you all finally sat back down in your seats to talk. Rajal asked more excellent questions. "Why does it implode when it hits the water? Why not before?" Oh my gosh. I wish you all would close your eyes and think. You are so close!

So many of you have a great attitude. I see you smiling when you make mistakes—or what you believe are mistakes. You're wanting to solve this problem so badly that you've forgotten about asking "Ms. Nac" questions. You are thinking and talking science and are enjoying it—or you're just great actors.

The bell rings and Jeff says, "I'll be ready with a plan for tomorrow."

Day 2

Jeff and Julia stand up and talk to the class as a whole. Jeff talks to them about the ideal gas law . . . Good job. You explained clearly what must be happening during the lab. Yes! Somebody actually spent time on this lab at home! I'm impressed . . . You did some thinking and now you're sharing it with the class . . .

Jeff then clearly explained what each group should do in lab. After testing, each group should send a representative up front to put data on the board. The class got up and went to lab to do testing. Jeff mentioned to reconvene with 15 minutes left in class.

Our students show up illustrating that they actually own their learning experience. They spent time outside of class, without our prompting, going over *yesterday's* material in order to make *today's* class more efficient, effective, and meaningful. How incredible! How novel! They determined they had homework, and we didn't write it on the board!

The class is discussing and debating the ideal gas law and how it affects their experimentation. At this point, the teacher hasn't mentioned it to them at all. A general research finding reported in *Inquiry and the National Science Education Standards* (2000) claims that "Effective learning requires that students take control over their own learning," which is a prelude for becoming scientifically literate. So in this instance, our students are initiating and holding these types of conversations on their own. We have found that the frequency, depth, and focus of these conversations increases as the year progresses and as more freedom is given with each project. This is real science. The students are making connections between content and observations, developing modifiable, workable scientific models in their heads.

Day 3

The class discusses the data gathered from yesterday's tests. Immediately, people are hungry for enough information to fill in the gaps. Bart wants to know the results from the other five groups' tests. David asks the class for its opinion on whether or not more testing needs to be done by his group. Alex questions tap water vs. ice water. Rajal wants to picture why time affects the amount of crush. Elliot adds that the amount of water is a key variable. And then Jeff explains it all! Everyone's contributions—lab data, questions, statements, etc.—are wonderful. This is incredible. What happened outside of class time from yesterday to today? It all suddenly came together!

You then all tested the same "best-case" scenario to check to see if your conclusion on how to get the can to crush the most makes sense. A few of you stayed up front to prepare for the presentation, including Kierstyn, your class computer guru. I'm finished here . . . Great job!

The day after the class presentation to "Dr. Fox," we have a discussion with each of the classes that participated, asking how they thought the project went. We ask the students the following journal reflection questions: What do you think went well? What would you change for next time? What content questions do you have about the activity? We spend some time discussing their responses, plus we will get to read their responses when we collect journals again.

We also read our journal entries to the students so they can hear what we were thinking throughout the project. With these journal entries, it's fun to include student quotes. And to prepare them for upcoming class tasks, we provide them with feedback and helpful hints. From reading the journal, it's obvious that there are a number of things we could focus on. We pick the following "big-picture" items at the beginning of the year to get them started on the right foot. As the year progresses, we add some of the smaller details. The following feedback was used for both classes we've discussed. This was read, along with class-specific feedback that we felt appropriate.

Feedback for CanCo Lab

"Here is a list of hints that may help you for future projects. I suggest you record them and reread them before your next class task." Ms. Gallagher shares the following:

1. Safety! Always primary. Everyone should have this copied in his/her journal.
2. Reread project sheets right after I present the task. Then keep silent as a class for at least minutes. This serves two big purposes: the managers have a chance to think through class organization. And the rest of the class has a chance to think about how to accomplish the task. This piece of advice is critical! Read and keep quiet.
3. Planning is the key!
4. Homework is your responsibility! If I don't assign it, figure out what you need to do to help the group.
5. Stop and think! When you're confused or you think you've made a mistake, stop what you're doing, backtrack to where you're confused, and figure it out! Problem-solving skills!
6. Make sure you give feedback for questions that is lengthy enough to clear up all misconceptions, if you understand the material. Make sure you ask questions if you're still confused.
7. There's still some discussion about the discrepancy of work between members of the class. The people who step up to volunteer to do the "extra" things are already doing what it takes to rise above the masses, so to speak. If you don't do it now, when do you think it will happen? What magical day in the future will you show your stuff? But there's always going to be an unequal amount of work in any group of people. It's a fact of life. You need to come to terms with it and move on. Something else: if you want to learn this stuff, like how to do a computer presentation, then ask to learn! That's showing concern for the future of the group and your own future.
8. Make sure everyone has all the information in his/her journal from the entire lab. I saw people making photocopies to hand out. If you did, great! If you didn't, get going on that! You're all responsible for all the information.

Handout 8—CanCo Project

CanCo Position: We are looking to hire a scientific community that can prove that it is able to effectively and efficiently solve our technical research problems. You can prove your community's worth by solving the problem outlined below and giving a 20-minute maximum presentation to our company representative on the assigned deadline. We will supply one of our company's chemists to act as a consultant while you perform your experiments. S/he will only help when asked a question. S/he may not be able to answer all questions, but s/he will try.

CanCo Technical Problem: CanCo wants to combine the cleaning and crushing operations at our plant. We have found that we can both clean and crush a can by putting some water into it, heating it, and turning the can into a bath of tap water. We are looking to install a robotics system that would do this operation, but we need to know the following:

1. What variables affect the amount of can crush (i.e., the initial can volume minus final can volume)?
2. How do each of the variables listed in #1 affect the amount of can crush?
3. What conditions should we set for the process to obtain the maximum crush?
4. Is the process (with your proposed conditions from #3) reliable enough to always give at least 70% volume crush on all cans? Provide enough data to support your claim.

Your Quality Presentation: Due to the representative's limited time, your community's presentation of results will be limited to a maximum of twenty minutes on _____ (at the end of your class period). Your presentation will start at exactly _____. Your presentation needs to concisely answer the four questions outlined above (think about "effective communication" when preparing). On this date, please provide a hard copy of your community's presentation for Dr. Fox. Your community will be competing against _____ other companies for our future business.

CanCo Project Continued

Chemistry Class Stuff—Areas of Assessment
Community-Based (20 pts.)
Community Effort—(i.e., What will Ms. G./Mr. S. see?) [3]
Reliability of Data (Consistent? Accurate? Precise?) [3]
Completion of Each Task Requested by Representative? [3]
Presentation Quality (ranked against other communities)—
    Remember this is a competition! Make it impressive! [8]
Focus on Safety [3]
Individual-Based (20 pts.)
    Role-Play (In character? Constructive use of class time? Acting
        as constructive member of scientific community?) [5]
    Contribution/Effort [5]
    Personal Understanding of Collected Data and Community's
        Presentation of Results—i.e., quiz later [10]

Other: You'll have the lab at your disposal for two days
(_____). During the two days, I, Ms. Gallagher/Mr. Smithenry,
will be role-playing as CanCo company chemist, Ms./Mr. Nac. You can
ask this chemist about anything concerning the representative's
requests and the company's future robotics operation using the "heating with water" crushing method. You are in charge of this project.
Good planning! And good-bye!

Gas Unit—Class Assessment

OCT	Part. Nature of Matter & Gas Laws	Gases Assessment

Megan and Noah, class managers,
put the question on the overhead and read it out loud to the class. "Look
at the picture on the bulletin board of the 'crushed' train car. A group of
workers steam-cleaned the inside of the tank. The next morning it looked
like this. Explain how you think this happened (a minimum of three sentences). Use a series of pictures to illustrate your explanation."

Tania reminds the class to keep quiet for at least one minute. Four
seconds pass, and Megan and Noah are bombarded with ideas from the
class! Yikes! So much for the one-minute idea!

After every unit, we give our classes two tests. One test is an individual test, because each student needs to be accountable for the chemistry content. We also assign a class assessment. Once all the individual tests are turned in, we hand an overhead to the class managers, walk to the back of the room, and record what happens. The class response is to be turned in on one sheet of paper before the end of the hour. This journal entry describes the class test given at the end of our Gas Laws unit. The previous CanCo project was a lab done during this unit, which took three days. This class test will only take part of one period.

"Where's the picture of the crushed train car?" Zach asks.

Noah's next. "How many pictures do you think we need to draw in order to answer the question?"

"Do we have to explain our pictures in sentences, too?"

"Should we break up into groups?" Katherine suggests.

"Did we cover this during this unit? I don't remember anything about trains!" Hans adds. The class laughs.

"Oh, my gosh! You guys, we need to get organized," Jenny says.

Megan says loudly, "Everybody hold on! I cannot help us get through this if you don't raise hands! You've all got some good ideas, but please! Before I try to get through any of those questions, let's reread the sheet and keep quiet like Tania said. I need to think!"

It just takes one. One student needs to be verbal and confident enough to remind the class to think! And although it's only October during this class assessment, Megan remembered the most important part about working together—listening to each other by raising hands. We usually start off our class assessments with questions or simple, one-step demos. Giving them a lab for a class assessment after a test this early in the year can be so chaotic that it's unproductive.

After a minute, Megan says, "OK, who has a question? Who has an idea about where to go on this one? Raise your hands!"

"Isn't this kind of like the can crushing thing we just did?" Taylor asks.

"Yeah, I think you're right," David concurs.

"Me, too," Sam adds.

"Wait. I don't get the picture. How do you know it's like the cans?" Irina asks.

"I think I can draw this," Paula offers.

"I've got something here, too," Matt adds.

"OK, we've got 15 minutes left. Let's talk about this as a class. I'll write your thoughts and draw your pictures on the board. You tell me what you think," Megan says.

The class works together for a couple minutes, but then side conversations start up. Thoughts are being thrown on the board, but the whole class is not following what is being written. Katherine has the "class" sheet and is copying stuff down.

Of course, there is still quite a bit of disorganization with these early assessments. For example:

- Does the class know what information is being recorded on the "class" sheet?
- Do they all agree with the "class" response?
- Would it have been better if they had worked in their six cooperative work groups, come up with a small-group response, and then shared together as a class?

The previous CanCo feedback did address how to handle some of these problems. We watch to see whether the class learns from this feedback. However, there is a new element of pressure in that they must finish this assignment in less than a class period. They don't have the luxury of going home to figure anything out. We'll discuss these new thoughts, along with the old, during feedback.

Although it's difficult to watch this chaos, it's a wonderful feeling for us that the chaos is actually rooted in the students' excitement to accomplish the given task. And they also feel a bit of time pressure. We give the class about twenty-five minutes to answer this "train" question. At the bell, the paper with their class response needs to be in our hand. That's the deadline!

"We only have one minute left. Who's got the paper? She's holding her hand out waiting for it! Hurry!" Sam panics.

Then a relay occurs. Sebastian hands the paper to Hans. Hans jumps a desk and runs to the back of the room toward me.

"Five, four, three . . . " the class yells.

I start backing away from Hans as a joke. The class laughs. Hans darts forward and throws the paper in my hand.

"Oh, my God, that was tense. I'm outta here!" Tania says with a smile.

Students start approaching me after class to ask, "How do you think that went?"

I tell them, "You'll have to wait for my thoughts till tomorrow. Think through what your thoughts are and bring them to class."

"You mean, you won't say anything now?"

"Nope! See you tomorrow!"

Our feedback for these class assessments is given the following class day. We give the students their individual tests back and then go over the content from the class test. We talk through their thoughts, see if anyone has anything to add now that they've had a day to think about the problem, and we draw particulate level pictures of what's going on in the train car. We also ask the students to write a journal entry answering the following:

1. Overall, how did you feel when you left the room yesterday?
2. What do you suggest the class change in order to improve for the next class assessment?
3. What did you do as an individual to contribute to the group or class task?

And then we talk. We give them suggestions for future class tasks, similar to those seen previously. We try to focus on three or four things for a particular class to improve for next time. These are unique to each class, as they will have different things to work on. We also share everything we shared with the other classes, so that everyone has the same advantage. So if another class did something very clever, or really got off-task and didn't do well as all, we share that along with our suggestions.

Stoichiometry Class Assessment

	Reactions &	Stoich.
DEC	Stoich.	Assessment

This next assessment is much more complex than the last example and much heavier in terms of data collection, analysis, and chemistry content. It's about five weeks past the time they had their gas law assessment. They've obviously been working in groups and as a class since this test. In November, they have had one class lab, a group project, and one class assessment. So they've added to their many experiences working as a class with little teacher direction from October to this point in the year.

The key addition in this assessment is more challenging content. We're adding one more twist. They still need to practice working as a group, but now need to critically think through much tougher concepts while doing so. An overhead is given to the class managers following the individual stoichiometry test. (See Handout 9—What Is This Metal?—at the end of this section.)

> Hal, a class manager, reads the problem aloud. The class keeps quiet for forty-five seconds or so. Becca yells out, "It's magnesium, right?" looking at the rest of the class. Most concur, so they answer #1 right away. They then watch me perform the initial demonstration of burning the metal sample.
>
> "OK, yeah, so it is magnesium. Did you see the bright light?" Scott says. "So now let's tell Ms. Gallagher what she needs to do for us."
>
> Hands begin shooting in the air. Hal calls on his classmates one at a time as Becca records questions and comments on the board.
>
> "Well, what data do we need?" Erica asks.
>
> "We need the mass of the crucible."
>
> "We need the mass of the magnesium."
>
> "We're not sure it's magnesium, dork." The class laughs.
>
> "Don't we need to know the mass of the stuff after it's done burning?"
>
> "Aren't we supposed to write a balanced equation?"
>
> Becca becomes the voice of reason and says, "Let's put down everything we know about this reaction on the board just to make sure we know what data to collect before we tell her what to do."
>
> I'm standing in front of the room listening to the students "talk chemistry." I'm smiling on the inside because this discussion is being led completely by the class managers and the inertia of the class's desire to solve this difficult puzzle. There are no side conversations about the individual test they just took. Everyone is focused on "metal X."

The discussion is genuine. They own the problem and want to figure it out. There's been a drastic improvement in the flow of the room since our October class assessment. Notice the increase in both organizational and content focus. The class is raising hands so that information can be recorded on the board and in every journal. The students are guiding one another through the problem and not allowing the room to become chaotic, even though the feeling of confusion exists in the room. They think before acting. And they've instinctively realized that we won't give them a problem that they can't handle. They're more comfortable being in charge and accepting challenges at this point in the year.

One area of improvement that is still needed is time management. They panic when they realize only a few minutes of class remain and they still need to record their thoughts on the class sheet. We address this in our feedback the next day.

Handout 9—What Is This Metal?

1. Based on your past experiences and on the initial lab demo I perform today, what do you think the identity of "metal X" is? A quick hypothesis, please.
2. Given the hints below as well as asking me to obtain the necessary data from the second demo, your task now is to mathematically prove or disprove your response to #1. Based on your calculations, what is the identity of metal X? Show ALL work!

   - If the math proves that your response to #1 is true, you're finished because your experiences match your math.
   - If the math doesn't prove your response to #1, answer #3 below.

3. List two things that could've happened during the experiment that would prevent the math from matching your response for #1. Then prove mathematically that these two "unexpected circumstances" (that you've just listed) were justifiable reasons for your different answers in #1 and #2.

   (Example: IF blah, blah, blah happened . . . , THEN our math would show blank . . . THUS, the identity would calculate to be . . .)

Hints:

    a. Metal X is a member of the alkaline earth metal family.
    b. You'll need to use conservation of mass law in order to do the calculations.

c. The product is from a synthesis reaction.

d. In the end, the molar mass of X might be important . . .

Thermochemistry Class Assessment

FEB	Equilibrium & Thermochemistry	Thermo. Assessment

We've now progressed to February. As always, they've been building their scientific community along the way and have become closer, as friends and as scientists. They're starting to really learn each other's strengths and weaknesses, helping each other when necessary.

After all the individual thermochemistry tests have been turned in, we give the class managers the overhead with the question that the class needs to answer. There are thirty-five minutes of class time left. The overhead has the following information:

> You make a 2.0 M solution of NaOH. The temperature of the water before you added the NaOH was room temperature. The temperature of the bottle felt warm to touch immediately after you dissolved the NaOH in the water. You put a lid on the bottle and leave the room. The next day, you can't take the lid off. It's stuck. Draw a series picture that explains at the particulate level why the lid won't come off. Use at least four sentences to explain your pictures.
>
> Young reads the cover sheet and overhead. Nice job. You did it quickly, which is good.
>
> Silence is happening, and Cam and Young talk about what to do. Good! After the silence, Cam tells the class that each group will draw a model of why they think the lid won't come off. Excellent! First of all, you came up with a good system. And you told the class, you didn't ask the class. Young then tells the class they have twenty minutes. Great! But did everyone hear that and does each group have a time-keeper? You're obviously saving the last ten minutes to talk as a class.
>
> I hear great discussions about bonds breaking and what happens with energy. Nice! I see some students looking for info in their journals and texts. Yes, energy is needed for a bond to break. And yes, energy is released once a bond is formed . . . How does this relate to the lid not coming off?

With only ten minutes left the class got together to share their models. Each group sent a representative to draw their pictures on the board. Once all six pictures were up, each group's representative explained its picture to the rest of the class. Good for you, Dave. In your model, you related the movement of the particles to the pressure above the liquid's surface! Wow! Your brain had to go back to October to do that! And you did a nice job of explaining it to the class.

After all six explanations were heard, the managers helped the class compare the models and decide on the best class response. Nice choice for class organization. Other classes have tried to do this as a large group and it wasn't as successful.

Our focus here is to synthesize chemistry content learned throughout the year. These assessments provide the platform for which to do so. It's impressive to see the students using their journals as resources. The pictures that they drew way back in October are useful to them now. They mean something to them. They realize that the gas law content is not learned in a vacuum, but rather is waiting to be applied to this new situation. They're making the connection!

FDA Investigation— An Acid/Base Project

MAR	*Acids & Bases*	*FDA Project*

"Good morning. My name is Dr. Woods (role-played by the teacher). I'm here as a representative from the FDA. Your company has been hired to determine the acetic acid content in three commercially available vinegars. Our standards state that the acetic acid content in vinegar sold to consumers must be 0.833 M ± 5.00%. I will be back in two days to hear your findings. Here is a printout of the contract directions. Thanks and good luck!"

The biggest difference between the CanCo lab (October) and the FDA Investigation lab (March) is that the latter project belongs entirely to the students. The students were still feeling their way with the bits of freedom we gave them during the October project. And remember there was a "consultant" available for questions at this time. There is minimal, if any, input from us during the March project because the students are prepared to act independently at this point. There is no consultant available. They're ready at this point to rely on one another to accomplish a task. And we give fewer details on the handout (see Handout 10—Is the Vinegar You're Using Safe?—shown at the end of this section). They've become very familiar with what is expected of their community. They've also learned to take things above and beyond what is expected, sometimes bringing in food for the representative hearing the presentation! Always a bonus!

The following is a journal from one of our classes during this March project. Notice the difference in organizational skills and ability to "fly" with the content. In this project, we sit in the back and type up what's happening. We do *not* role-play any character. Therefore, students must rely on each other for help. Certainly, if there is a safety hazard/violation taking place, we'll jump in. But other than that, this project is completely theirs.

Day 1

Dave and Young get up in front of the class. They tell everyone to reread the sheet they just received from "Dr. Woods." Then the class stays silent for one minute. Dave and Young are discussing what to do with the class. I see other people looking things up in different resources and still others writing things in journals. Great that you're quiet and thinking!

Once the silence is broken, safety hazards are read and recorded on the board right away. Good job, Mandy.

Jason rattles off the formula for acetic acid. Good. And Dave writes it on the board. Get properties of it, too. Yes, it is a weak acid. Nice thinking, Elena.

What concentration of NaOH should you use? Yes, you should think this through and calculate it. Great thinking, Allon! Young is looking at the materials in the back to see what quantity of NaOH I gave you to use. From here, you figure out what molarity to use. Then you calculate how to make it given the 500 mL volumetric flask. Great, Ron. Then Zach and Jason go to the back to make it. Then they return to the rest of the class discussion.

Dave assigns one vinegar to a lab group. Does the same with the other five vinegars to the remaining five lab groups. Tells everyone to do one trash trial and a minimum of four more titrations. Excellent.

The procedure for this is written on the board. I only see one person not writing this down in his journal! This is fabulous!

Time runs out. Dave tells everyone to reread the project sheet and to come to class understanding what test each group will do. Good! The manager gave you homework. Do it!

Day 2

Class comes in and some people have questions. Good! Make sure you ask them before going into lab. And I hear someone saying that she did research on the FDA. Fabulous! I can't wait to find out who that was! Good for you!

Yes, you should write your data down. Great reminder, Yuka. Where is the "master" copy of all the data that the class will collect? Where will you keep this? Who will keep it? Nice! Laura volunteers for this job.

I hear some students asking to use the Palms to gather data. Good idea. I see Dan and Helen connecting a couple of them to the cradles to collect pH data.

Hopefully everyone will use the same equipment for gathering data . . . "Spoke" too soon. Dave just mentioned that and made sure that all groups were doing so! Awesome!

While collecting data, I see great patience finding the endpoint. I see some group members actually performing the titrations while the others are doing some calculations and then giving the data to Laura. Great efficiency.

The lab is cleaned up and you reconvene up front to discuss the class data. Not much time is left . . .

A few people are panicking that there isn't much time left to discuss the presentation. Cam tells everyone to relax. Dan tells people to email him the information and he'll get it done in a PowerPoint™ presentation format. Dave wants to know which representative from each group will verbalize its findings. Sounds like you'll need to communicate outside of class to get this stuff done . . . We'll see what happens. But in terms of cooperation today in lab, it was fabulous!

Day 3

I walked to the classroom door with my "Dr. Woods" name tag on. Beth greeted me and offered me coffee. Everyone is dressed up and has a name tag. Good job! Beth showed me my seat. I was handed a hard-copy of the presentation.

Young and Dave gave the presentation . . . Company name was pH Productions Consulting . . . Hmm! Snoozeville. But honestly, most chemical companies have boring names . . .

Presentation was given in PowerPoint format. Nice!

Things covered: Objective, Standards, Procedure, Data.

Each vinegar discussed separately, which included graphs. Nicely done. Conclusion.

Way to go. You figured out the correct acid. It was "A" that fell out of the range.

And you all paid attention to the presentation!

Very smooth presentation. You sounded like you knew what you were talking about. The presentation looked like you knew what you were talking about. And you exuded that confidence I referred to last time. And nice work with the coffee and bagels, Beth. A smiling face and food never hurt!

After I left the room, I heard you applaud for yourselves, saying "Good job. Way to go!" Fantastic. You're there!

Feedback for FDA Investigation Lab

"Before I give you my feedback, I'd like to hear how you guys think you did. What did you think?" Ms. Gallagher asks.

"That was the best one we've done so far. We worked together and I feel everyone contributed something for the good of the group! That was fun!" Beth says.

Young adds, "I agree. Seems we really came together on this one. We had some disagreements, but in the end, everything worked out!"

"I agree wholeheartedly," Ms. Gallagher adds. "If you think back to where you were at the beginning of the year when working as a class . . . " (The class moans and smiles.) ". . . it's incredible how you've grown."

Beth says, "Yeah. I think it's especially neat that people feel comfortable doing what they are good at in order to make the product better. Some people are great at computer stuff. Some people are really good with the lab equipment. Some people really understand the chemistry and are open to explaining it to the rest of us. And, well, I know where to get good bagels!"

The class laughs. Ms. Gallagher adds, "Beth you do a lot more than just get good food. But I agree; those were good bagels! Now here are my thoughts."

"Wait, Ms. G., I have a question. Were you mad at us?" Ron asks. "I would look back at you during the project and you looked like you were mad at us, or that we were doing something wrong."

The whole class laughs and agrees with Ron. But Ms. Gallagher reassures the class, "I thought that's what you might be thinking! No, I was not mad at you. I purposefully try to keep a straight face while I'm typing up my observations of class. I don't want to inadvertently give anything away. Apparently—I've been told this by previous classes—my attempt to keep a straight face usually ends up as a scowl!"

We all laugh.

"Now, we're just about to embark on the long, end-of-the-year project I mentioned a while back. So here are my last thoughts and hints for you."

1. Nice touch with the coffee and bagels. Great idea to have some-one greet me and to show me to my seat. Loved the fact that everyone in class was dressed up, not just the presenters.

2. Looked like everyone felt part of the work and felt proud of the outcome. Good.

3. Make sure everyone feels comfortable with the content. Remember, the "representative" who comes to hear your pre-sentation could potentially ask any member of your company a question, not just the presenters—hint for next time.

4. Stop trying to read my expressions! When I'm sitting in the back, watching you and typing, sometimes I think you try to interpret how well or how poorly things are going based on a quick glance in my direction. Bad idea! I'm purposefully trying to keep a straight face! I'm not mad at you.

5. What could have been done before the second day of class? I was so happy to see that these little things were done as homework the night before. At least a few people thought to do them!

   - Calculations of +/- 5% of acetic acid
   - Procedure for titrations
   - Other: FDA research! Wow!

6. Label the containers!

7. Overall, the three main ingredients went really well for this pro-ject. You worked well together, your hardcopy report was detailed and accurate, and your presentation was smooth, confi-dent, and professional.

"So nice job! I'm glad you clapped for yourselves when "Dr. Woods" walked out of the room. You should be very proud of what you've accomplished. Let me reiterate one final piece of advice that I've been sharing with you all year. This will really help you during your final project. Remember that it's OK to be confused. It's what you do during those moments of confusion that matter! You know what to do, so don't forget. Don't ever let your frustration get the better of you. As a colleague of mine shared with me once, 'When you're really frustrated, look out! You're just about to learn something!'"

If you compare the feedback given for the October CanCo project to the feedback given for this project, you'll see a big difference. In October we know that the students need more hints on the "mechanics" of working as a class with minimal "teacher" input. They've never really done this type of thing before. In March, they have really "stepped out of the box," have shown their many talents, and are eager to take their work one step further. So they're looking for the little details that make the work superb, as opposed to just adequate. And we can tell that they are legitimately proud of what they've accomplished, because they did it.

We now have one final class assessment to share with you, one that concludes our acid/base unit. It follows this FDA lab by about a week.

Handout 10—Is the Vinegar You're Using Safe?

Background

The FDA has it under good authority, mainly that the director's daughter burned her mouth while eating a salad, that there are some commercially available vinegars that are not meeting FDA standards. All vinegars sold to consumers must, by law, contain 0.833 M $\pm$ 5.00% acetic acid.

Task

The FDA is looking for a scientific community that will determine which of the commercially available vinegars is outside the "safe" range mentioned above. The community who does the best job of investigating this danger, reporting its accurate findings to Dr. Woods, will be assured at least ten future contracts with the FDA. Your company will be given six solutions to determine their acetic acid content. Do this by titrating with an NaOH solution of your choice (which means you must prepare it) and using the indicator phenolphthalein. Good luck!

Minimum report information

Each company must submit a report that has as a minimum the following information. Anything else included in your report is up to you and your company.

1. Details of your procedure and your collected data. Collect enough data to *prove* your conclusion(s).
2. What is the concentration of acetic acid found in each of the six samples? Show calculations.
3. What is the pH of each sample? Show calculations.
4. Conclusion.

Presentation

At least one representative, Dr. Woods, from the FDA will be here on _____ to hear a presentation of your findings. S/he will be here at the beginning of the hour, so be prepared to start your presentation ASAP. And remember, other companies have been contracted out to perform these same tests. The company that best impresses the FDA representative will receive future contracts from us.

Acids/Bases Class Assessment

MAR	Acids & Bases	Acids/Bases Assessment

I am standing at the front lab table with a multitude of chemistry equipment at my disposal: pH meter, buret, buret clamp, beakers, Erlenmeyer flasks, phenolphthalein, 2.0 M NaOH, 2.0 M KOH, 2.0 M NH_3, balance, graduated cylinder, volumetric flasks, and an unknown weak acid.

I tell the class, "Today's task is to identify the unknown weak acid. But we're going to do this a bit differently this time. Pretend there is an invisible room around me and my chemistry equipment. I have equipped this pretend room with an 'intercom' system that will recognize only the voice of the name of the student randomly displayed on this computer screen. There are thirty minutes left in class. I will collect data for you for the next twenty-five minutes based on the instructions given by the 'recognized' student using the following parameters. The 'recognized' student can give only a one-sentence description like: 'Fill the buret with 2.0 M NaOH' or 'Use the pH meter to determine the pH of the weak acid solution.' An example of a sentence that I would not respond to is: 'Tell us the identity of the weak acid.' Once you believe that you know the identity and you have proof to support your claim, tell me to step out of the box and return as your teacher. At that point, the computer will select one more random student to explain the class' answer." I put the first student name up on the computer screen.

This particular class assessment throws a lot of it together: class organization, chemistry content, time constraint, and the challenge of problem solving. It also requires them to focus more on communication. They really have to listen to each other's suggestions and then distill that into one decision in order to tell the teacher what to do next. There is a bit of pressure on them to do things accurately, as well. If they formulate a poor decision, then the next 'recognized' student will have to correct that mistake. And it reiterates the importance of *every* community member pulling his/her weight in accomplishing the class task. Everyone has something worthwhile to offer the community.

And lastly, this assessment is so open-ended that the students really need to stop and think about what they've learned and how this will help them determine an appropriate response to the task. If they don't recognize that the chemistry concept of pKa is key to determining the identity, then the data collected will serve no purpose. Thus they have to "think chemistry" to figure out the problem. And the only way this can happen is if they use the organizational skills learned throughout the year.

This section shared chronologically two multiday labs and four class assessments. Each time a class task is assigned, we build on the previous skills and chemistry content that the students have learned as a class. Most of the labs, activities, and assessments we've talked about in this book have been adapted from traditional teacher materials. We simply put the focus more on having the students be in charge of their learning experiences and running their own classroom. We also like to add some sort of industrial twist whenever the occasion arises, so that students get a better appreciation of all that surrounds a professional scientist's job.

We would like to provide a quick outline of lessons from our solutions unit (taught in the middle of the year), just to give you a sense of how we intersperse traditional teaching (with a twist) and inquiry-based lessons. This is a very brief outline that will hopefully give you a sense for how our students really take ownership of what's happening in the room. Remember, we realize that the examples we use are chemistry-oriented. If you teach another area of science, we feel that our explanations can easily be adapted for your area in terms of what the students can do in the classroom.

Solution Chemistry (Example Unit)

JAN	Stoich.	Solution Chemistry

Here we share a brief example of an entire unit that we cover in chemistry. We cover this unit midway through the year, around January. At this point in the year, the students have had a good deal of practice with working in groups and as a class. They are safety-trained (see Chapter 4). They have two students who are considered class managers, detailed previously, chosen in a class vote in September. These two students take over the organization of class whenever the teacher gives a class assignment. And they are very familiar with the class climate being one that requires a community effort to succeed.

Day 1—Workshop

A workshop is one type of collaborative group work. Students are broken up into groups of four. Every person in the group is responsible for researching and recording responses. And each member of the group has a unique job, as well. One is a reader who is responsible for getting everyone focused on the same question and reads it out loud while the group follows along. Another is a pacer who is responsible for keeping the group on task and moving forward in order to finish the workshop on time. A third person is a traveler. This person is allowed to travel to the other groups in the room in order to get help with a question. The traveler then brings back that information to the rest of his group. No traveler is allowed to ask the teacher a question until he has first sought the help of all other groups in the room. And the fourth member is the clarifier. Before each member of the group records a response in her journal, the clarifier repeats the consensus response to make sure everyone is on the right track and agrees.

Once the class is finished going through the questions in their respective groups, the class goes over the problems together. Each group is responsible for writing their answers to one (or a few) questions on a white board in order to show the class (or will simply give their responses verbally). Each group presents their responses and waits to see if the class has any questions. The teacher is to facilitate the discussion, leading the class in a constructive direction, but is not to give answers. This can take some time, but is beneficial in that it requires the students to analyze one another's responses until an appropriate model has been built.

For instance, if a student questions, "Is that the right answer?" while the class is going over responses, the teacher should not answer yes or no. Instead, the teacher can suggest to the class to find a source that gives credibility to the response just read. "Find me a resource that provides evidence that this answer is right or wrong."

Another example of how to direct the class through the workshop conclusion follows. Slight adjustments to the questioning can be made if the answer truly is wrong. But if it makes sense, the student may ask, "Is this answer right?"

The teacher says, "Is there any part of the model that you feel needs clarification?"

"No. It makes sense, I'm just checking."

The teacher asks the class, "Is there anyone who disagrees with the model we just developed?" No one disagrees. "So I think we should feel confident enough to move on. After all, that's what science is— enough of a consensus to feel comfortable with a model to move on."

Our example introductory workshop (Unit VII: Liquids and Solutions—Workshop 1) for our unit on solution chemistry follows. Sometimes workshop questions require research above and beyond the textbook, so we take the class to the library to do a workshop. Sometimes the questions will require a small lab activity, so the groups are allowed to work in lab as they need to. Regardless, the students will have read the chapter before a workshop, so they should have some background on the topic being covered.

Unit VII: Liquids and Solutions—Workshop 1

1. From our discussions in September, what is the definition of a liquid?
2. What is happening when a liquid evaporates? Draw a picture.
3. Explain what happens when a bottle of perfume is opened on one side of a room and it can be smelled on the other side of the room.
4. Define vapor pressure. Define equilibrium in terms of a liquid in a container.
5. What is boiling point? How is it related to vapor pressure?
6. What is the difference between evaporation and boiling?
7. In nuclear power plants, liquid water exists in the reactor at temperatures near 700°F. How is this possible?
8. What is a solution?
9. What factors affect the solubility of a substance?
10. One way to describe the concentration of a solution is through molarity. What is molarity?
11. Describe how to prepare a 1.0 M solution of NaOH in a 100 mL volumetric flask. (NaOH is purchased as a solid.) Have your traveler show me your response. You may be asked to prepare this at the end of the workshop.
12. Describe how to prepare a 1.0 M solution of HCl. (HCl is purchased as a 12 M solution.) Have your traveler show me your response. You may be asked to prepare this at the end of the workshop.
13. What are colligative properties?
14. How might the boiling point of water be affected if sugar is dissolved in it? Draw a picture.
15. How might the boiling point of water be affected if salt, NaCl, is dissolved in it? Draw a picture.

16. Describe the similarities and differences for problems 14 and 15.
17. What is molality? What is mole fraction?

Day 2 and Day 3—Solutions lab

We give the students the following lab to complete, allowing them two days to do so. The teacher reads the lab aloud, answers any introductory questions the students might have—those that would not give away the answer, of course, and then tells the class managers to come up front to facilitate. The first day is usually a planning day. The class brainstorms, they do the practice problem given on the lab and check each other's work, they write up a procedure, they check safety information, and they divide up the work. The second day is usually devoted to actually doing the lab.

Even though the students are very familiar with the inquiry and community-based climate, there is still a lot of direction given in this lab. Reading it, you can see we give organizational hints as to how to proceed as a group. However, the actual chemistry content is quite challenging and is the major focus of this lab.

Solutions Lab

Task: Calculate the percentage of each component of a mixture containing sodium carbonate and potassium iodide. The only other chemical available for your use is 0.5 M calcium chloride.

Safety: Look up the hazards for all three substances listed above. Make sure you also know proper disposal procedures.

Procedure: A detailed, step-by-step procedure must be written out in your journal. Every member of the class must have this written out before any one member is permitted in the lab. Perform one trial per lab group and then average your results in order to answer the task question.

Homework: (Write this in your journal, then recopy it on a separate sheet of paper. One per person! Due _____):

1. A chemist has a 5.00 g mixture of silver nitrate and potassium nitrate. To isolate the silver, excess 1.5 M HCl is added. The dry AgCl precipitate has a mass of 3.50 g. What was the percentage of $AgNO_3$ in the original mixture? Show ALL work, including units. What volume (in mL) of HCl should the chemist have added to make sure all the chloride ions precipitated out? (This is a good practice problem for you to try before the lab. As you're trying to solve the problem, you may want to think through how the chemist performed the lab, as well as write the net ionic equations as you go.)
2. List two other solutions that would precipitate out one of the starting two chemicals from your lab. Write the net ionic equations.
3. For this lab, how did I prepare the 0.5 M $CaCl_2$ solution? (*Hint:* You need to look at the bottle it's in!)
4. For this lab, write out the net ionic equation. What were the spectator ions?
5. Answer the task question. Show all work! Pictures might help you.

Day 4—Lab overview, minilecture and Workshop 2

On Day 4, we collect a lab from each student and then give them feedback on how things went. As explained previously in this section, we have graded the class on safety and community and will grade their content accuracy on an individual basis from the labs we just collected. The feedback on how well they worked together is an important part of the lab in that it gives them the direction for the next opportunity when they will work as a class again.

We then spend about ten minutes going through the math behind solutions chemistry, in particular Raoult's Law, with a review on mole fraction and molality. The class then breaks into their small groups and works on the following workshop.

Unit VII: Liquids and Solutions—Workshop 2

1. Write the dissociation reactions for
   a. NaBr   b. $Mg(OH)_2$ c. $Al(C_2H_3O_2)_3$ d. $Pb(NO_3)_2$
2. Why are the colligative properties of an NaCl solution the same as an equally concentrated solution of KCl?

Raoult's Law Problems (Remember, there's a difference between ionizing and nonionizing solutes!)

3. What is the vapor pressure of a solution of 15.0 g of glucose dissolved in 15.0 g of water at 80.0°C?

4. What is the vapor pressure of a solution of 68.4 g sucrose dissolved in 90.00 g water at 80°C? at 100°C?

5. How would problem 4 change if the solute were 68.4 g of sodium carbonate? Show work!

6. Will the solution in problem 4 at 100°C boil? Explain your answer.

Calculating Boiling Points and Freezing Points

7. If 65.0 g of sucrose are dissolved in 392 g of water, what will be the boiling point and freezing point of the solution?

8. 50.0 g of $C_{10}H_8O_6S_2$ (a nonionizing solute) are dissolved in 100.0 g of water. What will the boiling point and freezing point of the solution be?

9. If 60.0 g of glucose are dissolved in 108.0 g of water, what will be the boiling point and freezing point of the solution?

10. If 54.8 g of nickel (II) bromide are dissolved in 224.0 g of water, what will be the bp and fp of the solution?

11. If 18.72 g of NaCl are dissolved in 75.0 g water, what will be the bp and fp of this solution?

12. If 34.44 g of $Ca(NO_3)_2$ dissolve in 72.0 g of water, what will the fp and bp be?

13. How would problems 8–13 change if the solvent was changed from water to something else?

Day 5—Freezing point depression lab

On Day 5, we spend time going over the workshop from Day 4, as described above. We also make ice cream! This, of course, is one of the students' favorite labs. It's also one of the most challenging. Although seemingly simplistic, when you get into the discussion about why the temperature of the ice actually decreased, the students will invariably discuss energy. This is a wonderful lead-in to our next unit on energy.

Freezing Point Depression Lab

READ THROUGH BEFORE DOING THE LAB.

- Each lab station is equipped with materials (except below) for the lab.
- Ice is in the middle lab station. Additives are up front.
- Clean up!

PROCEDURE:

1. Put ice into large resealable (or Ziploc) bag. Put enough in to cover the bottom of the bag thoroughly.
2. Record the temperature.
3. Put 0.5 cup milk, 0.25 tsp vanilla, 1.0 tbsp sugar into SMALL resealable bag and seal. Get all air out!
4. Place the sealed small bag into the large bag containing ice.
5. One person from each lab table should find out how much 6 tbsp of rock salt weighs. Then add 6 tbsp of rock salt to the large bag.
6. Seal the bag tightly and knead the ice bag by shifting side to side until the milk mixture reaches a thick ice cream appearance, about 5–7 minutes.
7. Record the temperature of the ice and salt mixture.
8. You may add treats to the bag from the front lab table. Please use sparingly so others will have some.
9. CLEAN UP THOROUGHLY!

QUESTIONS:

1. What were the initial and final temperatures of the ice/water?
2. Assuming you used 350 grams of ice/water, and assuming all the $CaCl_2$ dissolved, what would the new freezing point of the rock salt/water solution be? Show ALL work.
3. Explain at the particulate level why the $CaCl_2$ melts the ice.

Day 6—Individual and class test

Day 5 was used as a wrap-up for the unit. A day may be added or removed depending on your daily schedule. But once the previous activities are completed, the following day is assessment day. We give an individual test. We typically write an individual test that will take up half the period. We then present the class with one question that they are to answer together. The class managers facilitate. We step to the back and record what happens. An example of a question the students might see on a class assessment follows.

Liquids/Solutions Test   Class Period _____

- You may use each other, your journals, calculators, classroom materials (other than me), and your texts as resources. You may NOT leave the room.
- Answer the question on this sheet.
- Turn this in by the end of class.

1. $AgNO_3$, KOH, and $Pb(NO_3)_2$ are in three separate beakers as aqueous solutions. When mixed,

- Beakers 1 and 2 mixed = stays clear, no ppt.
- Beakers 2 and 3 mixed = turns white and cloudy
- Beakers 1 and 3 mixed = turns brown and cloudy

Which substance was in each beaker?

Beaker #1 = _____ Beaker #2 = _____Beaker #3 = _____

Justify your response in full sentences and show all net ionic equations.

And that's our solutions unit. Again, we hope you have a better picture of what our classes might look like in the middle of the year. We're still very much involved; however, the activities are student-centered. We're slowly allowing them to formulate the questions and determine the steps to solving a problem. There's limited direction from us as they take over. We develop the lessons so that students have little opportunity to just sit there. They're doing science. And more often than not, they're enjoying it!

Conclusion

"Oh, crap! Stand back! The pH is still 12!"

"Soap should be up on the front lab table right now!"

"Soap? Where do you see soap?"

"I'm the two-pound soap-makin' man. Give me that stirring rod and stand back."

"No. No. No. No. No. Pull that out of there. We don't stir with a thermometer!"

It's the last day of school. Our labs are cleaned and our desks our clear. We breathe a sigh of relief. Our work is done . . . until August, that is. We laugh together as we reread the student quotes that we recorded during the soap project. We also take some time to reread the student feedback about the project. One particular quote stands out: "The lessons learned from this project reached far beyond the arms of science. I will walk away with more from this project than any other before in my life."

"That's a good one to end the year on, wouldn't you say?" Joan says.

"Sure is," Dennis agrees. "Are you ready to go?"

We head to a restaurant to celebrate both our upcoming summer break with our colleagues and another successful end to a school year. We reflect on how our classes experienced yet another outstanding soap project experience. We realize that in a week or two, we'll meet again to plan and revamp for next year. But for now, we celebrate.

And you will, too, if you focus on this question: Who's running your classroom? At the end of the year, ours is run by the students. And the way we reach this goal has been outlined in this book. We prepare the students for role-playing a legitimate industry by presenting them with projects that become more challenging throughout the year.

Colleagues in our districts and teachers around the world have asked to learn how we create our exciting classroom communities.

Upon hearing our stories and reading our printed articles, they too have successfully implemented our strategies into their classrooms. Our purpose in writing this book has been to reach a wider audience to affect a greater positive change in creating science classrooms that truly incorporate inquiry-based learning. We want you to give your students the opportunity to do science.

No teacher wants a room full of robotic learners. If you share the innovative classroom vision bulleted in the introduction of this book, then take our challenge and slowly, methodically, and purposefully hand the reins over to the students. You'll be amazed at what a couple dozen high school science students can accomplish if you get out of their way and let them run the classroom!

Suggested Reading

(These resources will provide further background on journaling, collaborative group work, and the constructivist theory. They do not necessarily provide examples for how to implement them in the holistic approach used in our book. But they give you a start.)

Bransford, John D., Ann L. Brown, and Rodney R. Cocking (1999). *How People Learn: Brain, Mind, Experience, and School.* Washington, D.C.: National Academy Press.

Bromley, Karen (1993). *Journaling: Engagements in Reading, Writing, and Thinking.* New York, NY: Scholastic, Inc.

Burniske, R. W. (1994). "Creating Dialogue: Teacher Response to Journal Writing." *English Journal,* 83(4), 84–87.

Cohen, Elizabeth G. (1994). *Designing Groupwork.* New York, NY: Teachers College Press.

Johnson, David W., Roger T. Johnson, and Edythe Johnson Holubec (1990). *Circles of Learning: Cooperation in the Classroom.* Edina, MN: Interaction Book Company.

Jones, Gary (1990). "Last Laughs with Journal Writing." *New Mexico English Journal,* 5(2), 22–24.

Kohn, Alfie (2000). *The Case Against Standardized Testing: Raising the Scores, Ruining the Schools.* Portsmouth, NH: Heinemann.

Kohn, Alfie (1999). *The Schools Our Children Deserve: Moving Beyond Traditional Classrooms and "Tougher Standards."* Boston: Houghton-Mifflin.

Marzano, Robert, Debra Pickering, and Jane Pollock (2001). *Classroom Instruction That Works.* Alexandria, VA: Association for Supervision and Curriculum Development.

Mink, Joanna (1988). "Integrating Reading, Writing, and Learning Theory." Paper presented at the Conference on College Composition and Communication (St. Louis).

Schmuck, Richard A., and Patricia A. Schmuck (1992). *Group Processes in the Classroom.* Dubuque, IA: Wm. C. Brown Publishers.

Simpson, Mary K. (1986). "A Teacher's Gift: Oral Reading and the Reading-Response Journal." *Journal of Reading*, 30(1), 45–50.

Young, Art, and Toby Fulwiler (1986). *Writing Across the Disciplines.* Portsmouth, NH: Heinemann.

Zemelman, Steven, Harvey Daniels, and Arthur Hyde (1993). *Best Practice.* Portsmouth, NH: Heinemann.

Bibliography

Bolos, Joan and Dennis Smithenry (1996). "Chemistry Incorporated." The Science Teacher, 63(7), 48–52.

Bolos, Joan and Dennis Smithenry (1997). "Creating a Scientific Community." The Science Teacher, 64(8), 44–45.

Doris, Ellen (1991). *Doing What Scientists Do.* Portsmouth, NH: Heinemann.

Friedl, Alfred E. (1997). *Teaching Science to Children.* New York: McGraw-Hill, Inc.

Heywood, J. and S. Heywood (1992*). The Training of Student-Teachers in Discovery Methods of Instruction and Learning.* (No. 1/92) ED 358 034. Dublin, Ireland: Department of Teacher Education, The University of Dublin.

Krajcik, Joseph, Charlene Czerniak, and Carl Berger (1999*). Teaching Children Science.* New York: McGraw-Hill College.

Layman, John W. (1996). *Inquiry and Learning.* New York: College Entrance Examination Board.

Martin, David Jerner (2000). *Elementary Science Methods: A Constructivist Approach.* Belmont, CA: Wadsworth, Inc.

Monk, Martin, and Jonathan Osbourne, eds. (2000). *Good Practice in Science Teaching.* Philadelphia: Open University Press.

National Research Council (2000). *Inquiry and the National Science Education Standards.* Washington D.C.: National Academy Press.

National Research Council (1996). *National Science Education Standards.* Washington, D.C.: National Academy Press.

Ogborn, Jon, et al. (1996). *Explaining Science in the Classroom.* Philadelphia: Open University Press.

Rutherford, F. James, and Andrew Ahlgren (1990). Science for all Americans. New York: Oxford University Press.

Schmidt, W. H., C. C. McKnight, and S. A. Raizen (1997). *Splintered Vision: An Investigation of U.S. Science and Mathematics Education.* Boston: Kluwer Academic Publishers.

Turner, Tony, and Wendy DiMarco (1998). *Learning to Teach Science in the Secondary School.* New York: Routledge.

Wallace, John, and William Louden, eds. (2002). *Dilemmas of Science Teaching.* New York: Routledge.

Wellington, Jerry (1994). *Secondary Science.* New York: Routlege.